Australia The Hard Way

AUSTRALIA
THE HARD WAY

by
DAVID PYLE
with photographs by the author

Lodestar Books

Published 2020 by
Lodestar Books
71 Boveney Road, London, SE23 3NL, United Kingdom

www.lodestarbooks.com

A CIP catalogue record for this book
is available from the British Library

ISBN 978-1-907206-48-1

Typeset by Lodestar Books in Equity

Printed in the UK by Gomer Press Ltd

All papers used by Lodestar Books
are sourced responsibly

MIX
Paper from
responsible sources
FSC® C114687
FSC
www.fsc.org

Looking Back

Now coming up to my 77th birthday and with this reprint of my book, first published in 1972, I look back and think, why did we do this voyage in an eighteen-foot open boat? When I set off with Dave Derrick I was in my mid-20s; I had already sailed a Wayfarer dinghy across the English Channel and on the return passage broke the record for the fastest Channel crossing (with the help of a south westerly gale) in a sailing dinghy from Barfleur to Bembridge. A year later I entered my home designed and built ketch in the Singlehanded Trans Atlantic Race.

Basically I foolishly thought that I was indestructible and capable of sailing a Drascombe Lugger halfway around the world. The reason, I thought then, was to prove that it could be done, and that due to the type and size of this vessel our route would take us through countries, rivers, remote places and harbours that no other vessel could reach, and basically this is what we achieved. There were many occasions when we thought our lives were in serious danger of coming to an end, but someone or something fortunately decided otherwise – for which we were and still are eternally grateful. Maybe, when I am too old to sail my present yacht, I might be seen sitting on a bollard in some nearby harbour, a pipe in my mouth, splicing some rope and boring my grandchildren while I tell them yet again the tale of *Australia the Hard Way*.

David Pyle
January 2020

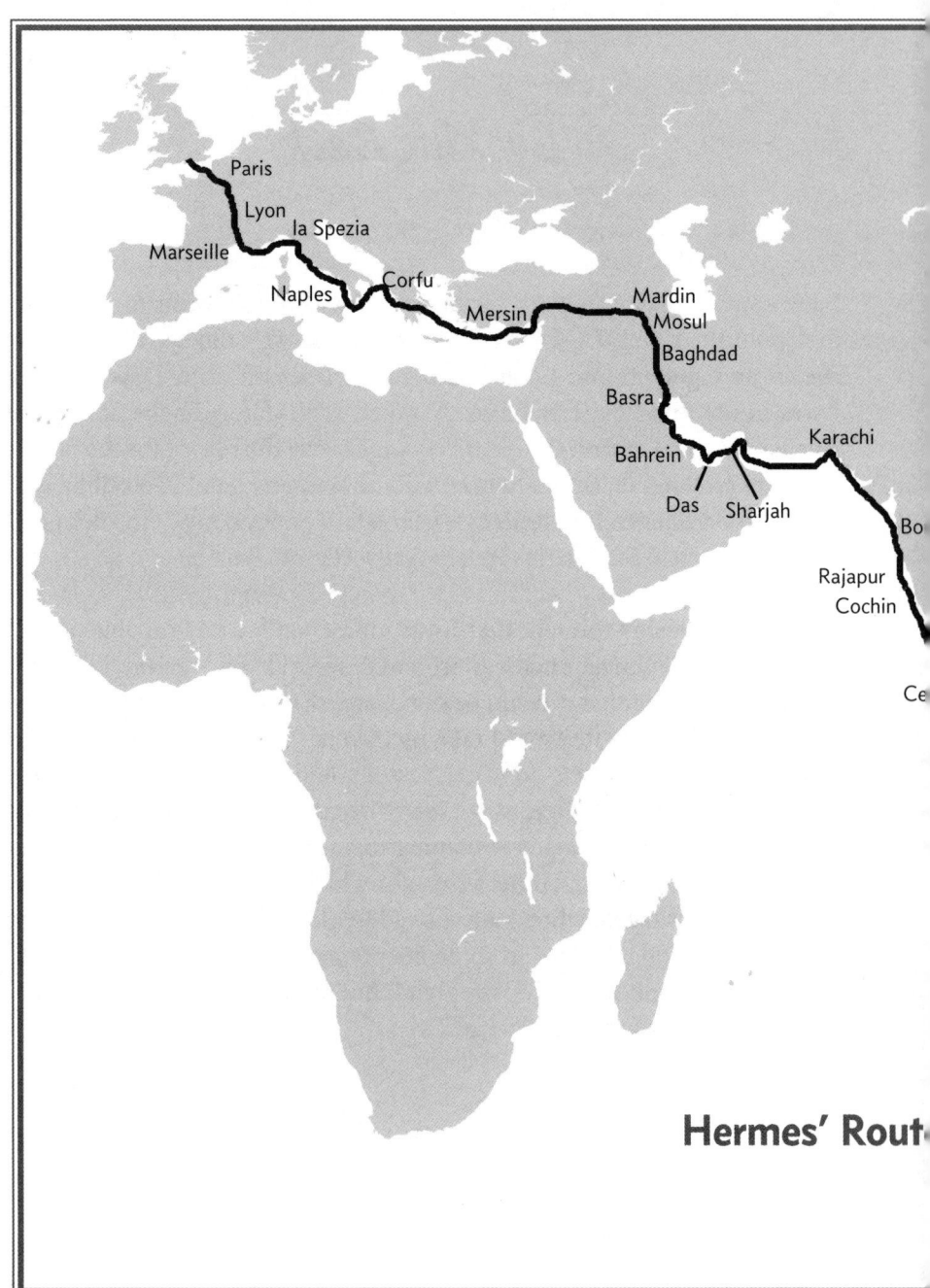

Hermes' Rout

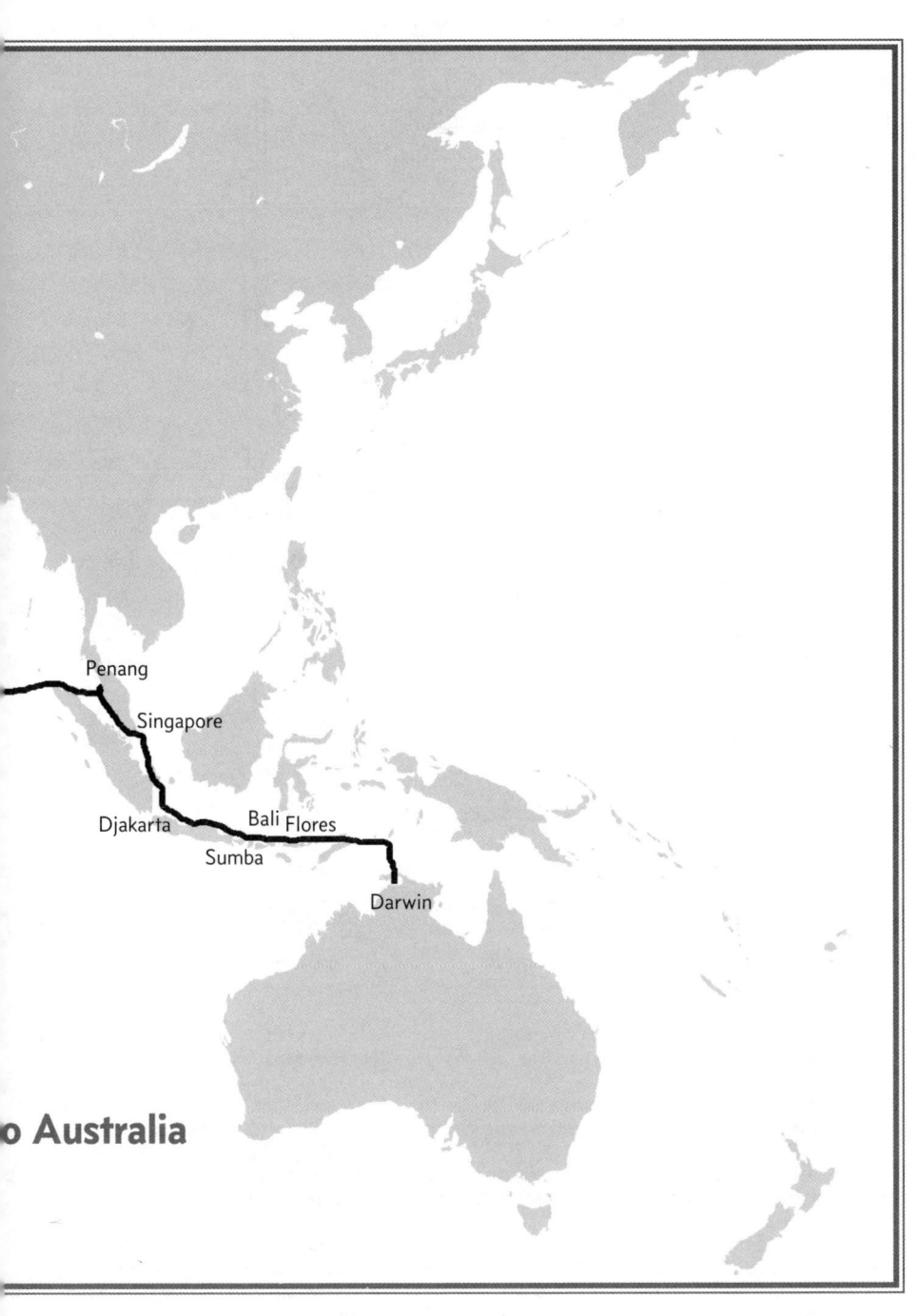

Penang

Singapore

Djakarta

Bali Flores

Sumba

Darwin

o Australia

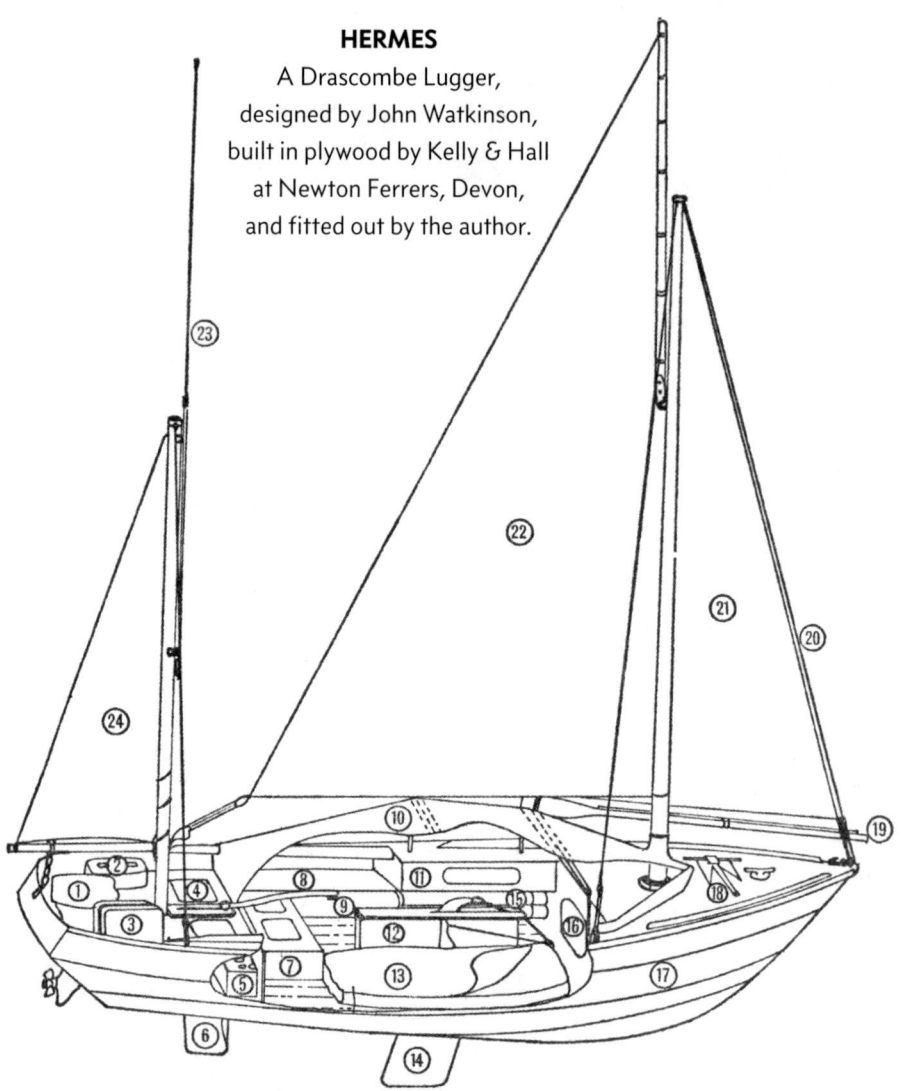

HERMES

A Drascombe Lugger,
designed by John Watkinson,
built in plywood by Kelly & Hall
at Newton Ferrers, Devon,
and fitted out by the author.

(1) Mercury 7·5 h.p. outboard motor. (2) Five-gallon fuel tank. (3) R.F.D. four-man life rafts. (4) Watertight hatches, port and starboard. (5) Two 12-volt heavy-duty lead-acid batteries, for radio and navigation lights. (6) $\frac{1}{4}$-inch steel spade rudder. (7) 'Sailor' radio transmitter and receiver in watertight box. (8) Tiller. (9) 14-gallon polythene water-tank, port and starboard. (10) P.V.C. nylon canopy. (11) Locker, port and starboard, for food and navigation equipment. (12) Centreboard case. (13) Air bed and sleeping bag. (14) $\frac{1}{2}$-inch steel centre plate. (15) Two watertight polythene tubes, port and starboard, for food and charts. (16) Water-tight hatch to forward locker for stowage of sails, clothing and perishables. (17) Hull of $\frac{3}{8}$-inch marine plywood, wide plank clinker construction. (18) Anchor. (19) Oars and whisker poles lashed onto forestays and shrouds, port and starboard. (20) Twin stainless steel forestays. (21) Jib. (22) Mainsail, loose-footed gunter. (23) Fibre-glass whip aerial for transmitter and receiver. (24) Mizzen sail.

Photographs

1

THE BOSS LEANED BACK IN HIS CHAIR. Clutching the bowl of his favourite Dunhill pipe in his right hand, he stared out of the window into the chill March sunshine.

'It's a crazy idea,' he drawled. 'You must be out of your mind.'

Commander John Wingate, DSO, had spent most of the Second World War in one of the Royal Navy's submarines, dropping commandos off the coast of France. Having retired in his late forties, he was now Warden of the Calshot Activity Centre on Southampton Water. I was 24, the youngest of his sailing instructors. Although we often disagreed, we were both professional seamen, sharing a deep respect for the sea and the English Channel in particular.

'I'm absolutely sure that a Wayfarer could sail across to France,' I argued. 'Just let me have one next weekend, over Easter. I'll prove it!'

Part of our job was to instruct youngsters from the county of Hampshire in the rudiments of sailing. We owned several of these small 16-foot racing dinghies, but only used them for pottering about close to the shore. From my own experience, I was confident that we could use them for cruising farther out, in the open sea—and I was determined to see the Centre expanding its activities in this direction. But to convince the boss was another matter.

'Of course I'll take full responsibility,' I added, 'I'll give you a letter, take out the insurance…'

'Very well, then. Take Vic Ruskin with you. But remember—I'll want a full itinerary, all properly set out in navy style.'

'Oh certainly. Thank you. Thank you, sir.'

I ran out of his office and down the corridor towards the staff room.

'Vic, mate, where are you? Vic, we're off!'

As chief sailing instructor, Vic was several years my senior. A slow grin spread over his lined, weatherbeaten face.

Owing to light head winds, we had to tack constantly; but thirty-six hours after leaving Calshot we sailed into Cherbourg harbour, feeling slightly smug. Our smugness disappeared rapidly when two harbour officials bore down on us.

'You have done a very stupid thing,' the senior of the two announced. His English was faultless; instinct told me that we were heading for trouble. 'Here in France we do not allow such boats more than two miles out from the harbour. For anyone to go farther out would be to risk suicide.'

'But we're English,' I replied, trying to conceal my opinion of French sailors. 'We go where we please. We don't bother with such regulations…'

'That may be so,' he interrupted curtly. 'But you are now in France. I shall have to refuse you permission to leave, or to sail more than two miles out from Cherbourg.'

We watched them walk away up the jetty, cursing roundly. I looked at the stupid slip of paper that the big fellow had given me. To stay was out of the question; apart from the boss wanting his boat back, we had to work for a living. 'We'll just have to slip out after dark,' I said to Vic, folding the paper carefully.

The small harbour of Barfleur lay some fifteen miles to the east. Drifting out of Cherbourg under cover of darkness, we stayed in Barfleur until the following morning. At mid-day I turned on our Pilot Pal, the small transistorised receiver that was our only means of contact with the outside world, for the shipping forecast from the BBC. For the Wight area they promised southerly winds, force five, which offered us a fast sail back. By early afternoon the French coast was receding into the distance; to play safe, I switched on the radio for the forecast again at five to two.

'Wight, Portland, Plymouth. Southerly gale force eight imminent…' the announcer intoned.

My heart missed a beat. 'Vic, did you hear that?'

'I wish I hadn't. How're we doing?'

'Barely a third of the way across.'

We donned oilskins in silence. Dark clouds, menacingly low, began to scud across the sky. By three o'clock the wind had increased to force seven, and ten-foot waves were beginning to throw our dinghy about like a cork. Having reduced sail to a small jib, we sailed on grimly, fighting each wave to hold our course. As we crested a big one, the white spume of spray stung our faces, but I thought that I caught a glimpse of St Catherine's Point on the Isle of Wight, its peaks jutting over the horizon, beckoning us on.

'Have to sail around the east of the island.' I had to scream to make myself heard above the wind. Thirty miles to go, and the gale was almost on us.

'Means another ten miles...' The rest of Vic's reply was lost in the howling wind.

But I knew that Hurst Narrows would be too rough, that we would be mad to try. We just had to hold on somehow, to avoid capsizing. No one knew where we were; we carried no life raft, no transmitter. Neither of us would survive in the sea for more than half an hour: it was too cold.

As we sped towards the Isle of Wight, the seas grew even more fearsome in size. The dinghy's designer had never visualised that two frightened men would face these short, sharp, steep waves in his boat. Clutching the helm until my knuckles were white, I prayed as I had never prayed before that I would be able to keep control.

Then it came: the one wave, larger, steeper, more vicious than all the others. The little craft rode up its back beautifully. But as we surfed down its face at a wild speed, she suddenly refused to answer the helm. We skidded on our beam ends in a wild broach; within seconds water was pouring in over the gunwales from the next wave. As I fought to regain control, Vic began to bail like a maniac with a bucket. We were too frightened to speak.

Somehow I managed to get her bows downwind again and we battled on. I still do not know how we survived the next hours. The strain on the helm was so intense that neither of us could manage more than half an hour before collapsing into the well of the boat, to spend the next 30 minutes grimly scooping the cold water out with the blue plastic bucket. Scoop up, over, scoop up, over she goes; I half-heard Vic shouting about how he would buy drinks all round if we ever got out of this mess. I never replied; I was too busy. Too frightened.

By nine o'clock, the island was only half a mile to the west. It was pitch black; as the wind continued to scream through the thin wire rigging, we saw the lights on shore beckoning us in. Ordinary people sitting quietly beside the fire, snug and warm. Just as I was beginning to think we were out of danger, I saw something white and ugly ahead.

'Waves breaking over something ahead…' Vic screamed at me.

'Rocks on Bembridge Ledge,' I yelled. 'My God—we're too far in.'

In desperation I pushed the helm hard over. Although I fought to sail back out to sea, the white foam of disaster crept menacingly nearer. We were being pushed in remorselessly, and could only hope that the tide, which was against us, would be strong enough to push us clear of the rocks. For ten long and lonely minutes we stared at the boiling cauldron, now a bare hundred yards off our port bow, transfixed in sheer terror.

We were swept around the rocks with about ten yards to spare. Half an hour later we beached the little boat on the sand in Bembridge harbour.

Before presenting ourselves in front of the boss next morning, we took care to scrub carefully and put on clean clothes. We sauntered in, for all the world as if we had just taken a gentle row on the Serpentine. 'Well, we made it,' I announced cheerfully. 'We even broke the record for a dinghy crossing. Ten hours. Not bad?'

Little did we know that the Warden had spent most of the previous night keeping watch for us, tight-lipped, from the cliff top. Instead of a pat on the back, we received the frosty reception that we richly deserved. 'So I see,' he said menacingly. 'That's the last time I intend to allow anyone to take off in one of my boats.'

Exit two record-breaking dinghy sailors, suitably chastened.

2

SAILING HAS ALWAYS DOMINATED MY LIFE; at the tender age of three, I remember that I was used as movable ballast. Our family sailing boat in those days was a Victory class, a deep-keeled, clinker-built Bermudan sloop that leaked like a sieve whenever the wind blew strongly enough for her to heel more than ten degrees. Most weekends and holidays in my early childhood were spent racing this sluggish old lady up and down the length of Portsmouth harbour, skilfully weaving our way through the mothballed Reserve Fleet. We always came in last.

By the time I was seven I was sailing with my brother Peter, three years my senior, in a nine-foot dinghy with a rag of a sail tied onto an old oar. She had been built by my father just after the war, from offcuts of half-inch elm bought from a heap of scrap wood at the Portsmouth naval dockyard. Nevertheless she was our boat; every winter we would haul her out of the water and paint her with loving care.

When we went away on holiday we usually camped, somewhere along the Devon coast. Periodically my brother and I would be shepherded towards the beach and taught how to swim. During the winter my primary school took over this essential task and I was soon able to do a whole length of the swimming baths. Lifejackets in those days were rarely used by dinghy sailors; they were far too large and clumsy to wear onboard a small boat. The dinghy sailor had to be able to swim.

A few weeks before my twelfth birthday, a very battered ten-foot dinghy arrived in our back garden. For the following few weekends and most evenings, my father could be seen busily sawing planks of wood and hammering away at this rotting hulk.

We lived at this time in a three-bedroomed house, designed by my father and built by two of my uncles, a mile from the waters of Chichester harbour. A 200-square-foot patch of barren land, just behind our garage, served as our private dinghy pen; this was cluttered during the winter with upwards of four dinghies of all shapes and sizes. Since my earliest days, our garage had always been occupied during the long winter months by some half-built boat, the floor knee-deep in spruce shavings and pieces of marine ply, while the car rusted outside on the drive. We often lost count of how many boats we had; early every summer the garage doors were opened and disgorged yet another. Most summer evenings my father could be seen at the drawing board; by the autumn a dozen eight-by-four sheets of marine plywood had arrived, and so the cycle began once more.

But my twelfth birthday was something very special—that little clinker-built dinghy, now painted a bright blue, was the first boat that I could call my own.

I wanted to give her an original name and spent hours poring through a variety of books on aquatic birds until I came upon the Latin word for swan—anatidae. The swan is one of the most beautiful and graceful birds to visit our small harbours and lakes. It seemed most suitable for my very first boat. A few days before her launching I carefully cut, sand-papered and varnished a short length of mahogany, painted *Anatidae* on it with black paint trimmed with gold, and screwed it onto her transom.

I had reached the exalted position, in my father's eyes, of having sufficient experience to sail on my own. When the season arrived two months later, *Anatidae* was equipped with a mast made from the inevitable oar, and a small red standing lug-sail. With most of my Post Office savings, the princely sum of £18, I bought a small one and a half horse-power outboard motor, ideal for exploring the intricate network of muddy creeks in Chichester harbour. We spent many days together exploring. We would face the perils of the sea, fighting off imaginary pirates and discovering new islands, and even whole continents, sleeping out under the dark star-studded sky, leading an idyllic life.

I knew that my mother often worried about my lone sailing jaunts, but I was too young to appreciate the extent of her feelings, though we were always very close. My brother Peter, a successful scholar with a good mathematical brain, had the ability to follow in father's footsteps as an engineer; naturally a better understanding developed between him and my father than with myself. I was no scholar. Perhaps there is always difficulty in a family where one of the sons turns out brilliant. But even if my father and I never established a very close relationship, there was still a strong bond between us.

I am afraid that my mother occasionally had cause to worry. One day during our first summer together I had been exploring farther afield than usual. The day was drawing to a close and I was on my way back to our sailing club. The wind was becoming uncomfortably strong, and with her little sail billowing out to one side, *Anatidae* surfed along on top of the increasing seas. Her bow would rise and dip into the crests showering a spray of water out on either side. When I looked around, I could see no other boat—we were alone and I was rapidly becoming very frightened.

At that point the main channel divided into two, and I had to take the left fork. This meant that I would have to gybe the sail across. By altering course, the wind would push the mainsail across to the other side; a dangerous manoeuvre in this wind, with a good chance of capsizing and my being cast into the cold grey water, which was an idea that I did not relish. I slowly brought the sail in, and put the helm over. The boom rose and dipped, then rose again. At its highest point, it flashed across to the other side with tremendous force. We heeled over at a sickening angle. Water gushed in over one side while I clambered frantically to the other. Slowly she settled back on to an even keel, completely awash. The land 100 yards to windward now gave me some shelter, and I slowly sailed on, bailing with an old rusted tin can as I went, realising that life in a little dinghy was not all like Arthur Ransome's *Swallows and Amazons*.

I rarely discussed my short, single-handed voyages in *Anatidae* with my mother, as I always feared that she would stop me from sailing off on my own. She would always tell me to be careful before I set off, not to do anything silly, but she would still cut and pack my sandwiches, a few pieces of home-baked cake and a flask of coffee.

Even in these early days, I was much more enthusiastic about exploring distant lands than racing. I felt that to sail off on my own was really the only way to learn what sailing and seamanship were all about. Finding out by trial and error helped me to gain the confidence and the ability to handle small craft much more quickly than under permanent instruction.

When I was fifteen I was sent off to boarding school for the last year of my schooling. I had been a day boy for four years, but my parents had now moved from the south coast to Manchester. The time had come: *Anatidae* had to be sold. She was the last boat that I would call my own for many years to come.

I left school at sixteen and a half, much to the delight of my principal. The masters had called me a dreamer, unable to settle down to any serious subject, and it was probably still as a dreamer that I signed on for twenty-two years as an apprentice surveyor in the Royal Artillery. It soon became evident that I was temperamentally un-suited to army life. I found the continuous spit and polish a bore, and my superiors irksome. The only benefit I gained was an introduction to the mountains, and I became very enthusiastic about rock climbing. After less than two years I decided to approach my commanding officer to see if I could buy myself out. I had definitely decided that I must leave.

Having been suitably briefed, I waited while the sergeant-major knocked on the CO's door. 'Come in,' came a plummy voice from inside. The door was opened, under the bellow of the sergeant-major I marched in six paces, wheeled to the right, marched three more and slammed my feet to a resounding halt. 'Pyle, Bombadier 23728146, sir.'

'Stand at ease.' A golden crown and two shining pips on each shoulder. 'Well, what is it, Pyle?'

'I wish to leave the army, sir,' I said, with determination.

'This is not Civvy Street, you know,' he said. 'You can't just hand in your notice. Why do you want to leave anyway?'

'I don't think the army is a suitable place to marry and raise children in, sir.'

'Good God, man, why not?'

'I don't like the class distinction which exists in the services, sir.'

'You're not a communist, are you?' he said, looking at me through narrow squinting eyes.

'I'm a socialist, sir.'

For a while he seemed stuck for a suitable reply. 'Very well, Pyle,' he mumbled, 'I'll see that your request goes through.'

Within a week I received a note from the commanding officer, giving me permission to buy myself out for £80. I must have impressed him during the interview, as the normal price for the time I had been in the Army was £100. He had given me a 20 per cent discount.

I was all of 18 years old at the time, but security meant a great deal to me. I wanted a life which would offer a stable future, not only for myself but for my wife, if ever I married. I was not in the running for university, although my educational qualifications had increased during my short service career.

Agriculture seemed to fit the bill, as well as offering an interesting open-air life. The idea of working in an office couldn't have appealed less and farming had been in my mind before I left school. I went to agricultural college, then spent a year in Denmark on a student exchange scheme to study their pig farming. When I returned in February 1964, I became a manager of an intensive pig farm close to the small village of Peasenhall in Suffolk. But the call of the sea and the mountains beckoned me once more.

For many months I thought seriously about leaving farming and going off as an instructor at an Outward Bound school. It would mean giving up an excellent job, even a house and a car of sorts, for the insecurity of working as a professional on the sea and in the mountains. Various girls had come and gone during my agricultural career, but my life was still my own.

I remember that I had a long talk with my father while I was still undecided. He was in one of his more benign moods. 'You're still young,' he said. 'Wouldn't it be better to get this urge for adventure and travel out of your system now, rather than wait until you are either too old, or tied down with the responsibility of a family. When I was your age, we were going through the depression, and our only object was to find work. But now there's work for the asking. You must do as you think best.'

I was faced with making what could turn out to be the most important decision of my life. During my spare time, at holidays and weekends, I would wander off to the mountains, instructing young people in climbing. But this was not enough. Through a pull that I could not identify, I knew that I had to make a living, for a time at least, from sailing and mountain-eering. So with some misgivings I gave three months' notice on the farm in December 1964.

My subsequent career with the Outward Bound Trust, at the Aberdo-vey Outward Bound Sea School, lasted almost a year. Then I moved from Wales to the Hampshire County Council's Activity Centre at Calshot on Southampton Water. I learned a lot there. It was 1966, and in two years' time the third Observer Single-Handed Trans-Atlantic Race was to take place. The idea of entering this race meant a great deal to me. I had to do something to establish myself in the world of yachting; to prove to myself that I was a good sailor and navigator. And I had something else in mind that would be an even greater challenge, something for which even the Trans-Atlantic Race would be merely a practice run.

To enter was no easy matter. I had no boat and very little money, but I was determined that I should be one of the competitors at the starting line. I would have to design a craft and build it from scratch; and that de-sign and method of construction would be dictated by the amount of mon-ey that I would be able to afford. I opted for a method that my father had been working upon for the past eight years, and together we sat down at the drawing board to produce a design that was suitable both for the race and for my pocket. The plan was to build her bit by bit, on the assumption that I could afford to buy a sheet of plywood or a few more screws every week. She was also designed for strength and every detail was thoroughly thought out, from the chain plates capable of taking a 25-ton load, to her ketch rig, easily handled by a single-handed sailor.

For the next year every spare moment was spent on building this 27-foot ketch. Evenings, weekends and holidays. With the exception of my fa-ther, I received little help and usually only scathing criticism. After I hand-ed in my notice at Calshot, John Wingate, the Warden, called me aside. 'I don't think you really ought to go ahead with this race,' he said. 'Why not leave it until you can afford a boat from a reputable builder?' It was obvi-ous that he, like most of my friends, thought that I would be sailing to my doom attempting to cross the Atlantic in this boat.

In July of 1967, *Atlantis III* (the third *Atlantis* within the family) was launched. During that summer, I set off for a 500-mile non-stop single-handed sail, to qualify for the Trans-Atlantic Race the following year. My course was to sail across to a buoy a few miles north of Cherbourg, then down to Ushant, a notorious group of rocky islands off the north-west corner of Brittany, then northwards to the Scilly Isles and back to Chichester harbour. After two days, having rounded CH 1, north of Cherbourg, I was tacking my way down the English Channel towards Ushant.

It was the first time I had been sailing single-handed offshore. Besides my being frightened at being so totally alone, Atlantis was giving me cause for worry. She was leaking badly up for'ard, and two or three times a day I would have to bail water by hand from a large for'ard compartment to the centre bilge area, where I could pump it out with the hand pump. Everything inside was damp, streaming with water, and cold. The only luxury on board was one bunk, six foot three long by two foot six wide, with a hard, cheap mattress. With all the work that I had to do below, I began to feel grossly seasick. The day was gloomy, with low, grey, scudding clouds whipping across the sky, and a fine drizzle. As the wind was on the increase, I reduced the sail to just a working jib and the mizzen; I was busy over the side, being disgustingly sick, when I looked up to see a large naval destroyer emerging out of the mist, slowly rolling her way westwards. The ratings on board were far from sympathetic, and gave a friendly, cheerful wave. I had never been too keen on the Services. My appreciation of them now sank to rock bottom.

The following night I was approaching Ushant, that rock-strewn corner of Brest where many a ship has foundered, when I noticed the lights of a ship heading directly for me. I turned on all the navigation lights, floodlights, and masthead lights to identify myself as a sailing boat, which, under Rule 20, established my right of way over motor vessels. The ship did not alter course, and continued directly towards me. I reached down for the powerful Aldis lamp, and shone its bright beam onto the sail to identify myself to the blindest man on watch. Still she steamed towards me. I put *Atlantis* about to sail away from her, since the ship was now very close; in a cold fury I flashed a morse signal onto the bridge, 'Fuck off.' At least this brought a response, in that a searchlight was shone onto *Atlantis* from the bridge. The massive great black hulk, with the sound of her engines rumbling deep in her bowels, steamed past with only 100 yards to spare. 'You're bloody stupid, blind idiots,' I yelled towards the dark shadowy outline of her bridge vanishing into the night.

I was within ten miles of Ushant—as close as I wanted to go. The weather was deteriorating, so I altered course for the Scilly Isles. The following morning I was fifty miles south of the Scillies with the wind now blowing near gale force. Rather than foundering on the towering granite cliffs of Land's End, if I carried on, I thought it prudent to alter course again and head back to the Solent which lay 200 miles to the east.

A full gale was now blowing from the south-west and I was becoming increasingly nervous at the thought of riding it out alone. With working jib and mizzen set, *Atlantis* was surfing along at seven to eight knots before the wind. I had no self-steering, but while beating down to Ushant, she managed to sail herself, with her sails trimmed. Running before the weather was a different matter. I realised that she would yaw badly one side or the other, with a tendency to broach, unless I stayed on the helm continuously. I had no option but to guide her all the way home.

For thirty very long, very weary and very cold hours I stayed in that cockpit. As I sailed alone through the night, the loom of the lighthouses of Start Point and Portland cast a ghostly glow over the horizon to the north, and I realised that I was becoming exceptionally weary. I could not go below to cook up a hot drink, let alone a hot meal.

This was by no means my first gale; earlier the same year, I had returned successfully from Barfleur with Vic. But it was still frightening, and lonely as well.

Dawn finally broke on *Atlantis*, and the daylight, although grey and overcast, gave me new life. By mid-day the gale had moderated and I rounded the Isle of Wight. As I sailed back into Chichester harbour, I realised that I had learned a lesson of endurance, for both myself and my boat. Past criticism now seemed completely unfounded.

Early the following year, after modifications had been carried out to Atlantis in the way of additional ballast and design of rig, I set off with two friends for the port of Den Helder, in north Holland. On the return voyage we encountered a severe gale in the North Sea. *Atlantis* survived the onslaught without any damage, but one of the crew, as soon as we arrived at Dover, left the ship's company rather abruptly. It made me wonder if I was completely incompatible as a skipper, in which case I had better stay with single-handed sailing. However, the other crew member, a girl, stayed with me as far as Chichester harbour—probably out of loyalty more than any love of sailing.

A week later, I set off in *Atlantis* from Chichester harbour bound for Plymouth and the start of the Trans-Atlantic Race. It was a wonder that I ever arrived. I spent the first day becalmed off the Isle of Wight. That night a wind came up from the south, and I sailed along the island's southern shore. As a matter of practice, I would always look carefully around for shipping and other dangers, set the alarm clock for half an hour, and then go below for a short sleep. On this occasion I overslept the alarm. Two hours later I came up into the cockpit just in time to prevent our being smashed on the rocky shores off St Catherine's.

Two days later I was in Lyme Bay, in thick fog, having spent the whole of the previous night drifting around in circles. Suddenly a small fishing boat loomed out of the mist and I hove to alongside her. 'Could you tell me the way to Start Point?' I asked, feeling rather embarrassed.

'Follow your nose,' he said, pointing into the mist. I took a rough bearing of the direction that he gave and set off once more. My navigation equipment was the very minimum required, a sextant, a compass and charts; unfortunately funds did not run to modern electronic equipment. Within two hours Start Point loomed up half a mile ahead, on the bow. Another four hours of good sailing and I was in Plymouth Sound. A week of last-minute preparations followed, until I was finally towed out towards the starting line on the calm, drizzly morning of 1 July 1968.

My parents were in the towing launch. When this came alongside I well remember how my father extended his hand: 'I don't think I've ever done this before, but the very best of luck!' I could see my mother forcing a brave smile, but worry was written all over her warm, gentle face. I confess that I shed a tear myself.

When the starting gun resounded across Plymouth Sound, thirty-five small yachts set off for America. My chances of winning were nil; few of us could compete against expensive ocean-racing yachts, some of nearly sixty feet, helped across by computer. I was out for the adventure and excitement. I gave a last wave to my parents in the launch, which had turned around by Plymouth breakwater, and settled down to the long voyage ahead.

3

FOR 17 DAYS I WAS BATTERED AND TOSSED in the gales of the North Atlantic. In one particularly bad blow my sails parted at the seams, the self-steering broke and my generator flooded. The batteries for the radio and lights were drained of the smallest spark. Then, to add to my troubles, one of my teeth broke, giving me days of excruciating pain. I had only one sensible choice to take, to head my battered craft for the Azores, 200 miles to the south, for repairs. Twenty-one days after leaving Plymouth, *Atlantis* and I sailed into the small harbour of Ponta ãDelgada in the Azores.

Ponta Delgada is a small man-made harbour built on the south side of the oceanic mountain of São Miguel, with steep slopes that plummet down into the sea and downwards for over two miles to the ocean bed. When the customs officials came on board, welcoming me to their little island, I greeted them with mixed emotions: I was bitterly disappointed because the race for me was over, but at the same time I was jubilant because my navigation had been perfect. After steering a very erratic course, with a broken self-steering system, I had found a mere pin-prick of an island in this vast North Atlantic Ocean.

I went ashore to arrange for the repair of my various pieces of equipment. The self-steering was broken beyond repair, and so was the charging motor. I took the batteries to a small garage for charging and the sails to a cobbler's to be sewn up and patched with thin strips of white leather. Neither asked for payment. The lives of the Portuguese on these islands are dominated by the raging North Atlantic and they readily sympathise with anyone who has suffered from its onslaught.

When I telephoned my parents in England from the main Post Office in Ponta Delgada informing them of my decision to return, my father was overcome with relief at hearing my voice. None of the ships that I had seen on voyage to the Azores had reported my position to Lloyd's, as I had requested, and so no one knew whether I was still alive or two miles down in the dark depths of the Atlantic. As I put the receiver down, I felt guilty for the first time: guilty at having entered the race in the first place, of thinking only of myself, my own pleasures and excitement, not of the possible grief that it might cause to others. I felt I must make every effort to return as soon as possible.

Two days after arriving in Ponta Delgada, I was as ready as I ever would be for tackling the 1200-mile voyage back to England. The sails were hoisted and we slipped out from the small harbour. With an afternoon sea breeze blowing from the south-east, we headed due north, to pick up the Atlantic trade winds which blew for 400 miles north of the Azores. For three days I sailed steadily and uneventfully northwards. On the third evening, however, dark heavy cumulus clouds began to form to the west and to roll in fast towards me. For most of the day a steep heavy swell had been running in from the west, so that I was expecting trouble. Trouble I got. For four long weary days I was smashed and battered with the pounding seas created by hurricane Brenda. *Atlantis* was battened down, every hatch clamped shut, while I sat below in the damp, dripping cabin.

While the hurricane blew, I tried to console myself with planning what I considered to be the ultimate voyage, the ultimate challenge. For two years I had been thinking of a voyage that would test to the utmost my skill of sailing, seamanship, navigation, and, by taking a crew, my ability to get on with other people. It was simply to sail a small open boat from England to Australia—halfway round the world, possibly the longest open-boat voyage ever. Before the hurricane had blown itself out, I had decided to sell *Atlantis* as soon as I arrived home, to plough all the money into this project and to leave England early the following summer. At the worst moments of this trip, when I thought *Atlantis* was going to be wrecked, my one hope was to salvage something for the next one.

On 28 July *Atlantis* and I sailed into Chichester harbour. My mother and father had seen me come through the harbour entrance, and came out to meet me in one of our small dinghies. They were obviously delighted to see me, but I was shocked to see how thin and ill my mother looked, so I decided to keep quiet about Australia for the time being.

But I did some hard thinking about the voyage and the route it would take. The Suez Canal was closed, and anyway the Red Sea was impractical for an open boat, at least in summer—the heat would be too great and the ports for taking on fresh water were too far apart for there not to be real danger of death by thirst and dehydration. The route via the Cape of Good Hope was too long, not just for an open boat but for my financial resources as well. Cape Horn, of course, was out of the question. That left a partly overland route—well, why not? If I could somehow get the boat carried through Turkey, then perhaps I could travel down the Tigris-Euphrates river system to the Persian Gulf. Closer examination of the charts showed that irrigation schemes and dams made the ancient river way of the Euphrates unnavigable. But the Tigris looked possible, and from there onwards the sea-voyages could be both short and feasible.

I put *Atlantis* up for sale, trying not to think of the happy times and adventures we had had together. Although I badly needed the money, I was secretly hoping that no one would buy her and that I would find the money some other way. It wasn't long before I began to receive answers to my advertisement; within a short time I found a buyer, a Mr Jones, inevitably from South Wales. Mr Jones seemed the sort of man who would take good care of her, who would not let her rot in some small creek. His intention was to sail her across the Atlantic to America where he was going to live, so I felt that she still had plenty of adventure ahead of her. When he handed me a cheque for £800, *Atlantis* and I parted company for the last time. The same evening I wrote to Kelly and Hall of Newton Ferrers in South Devon, to ask if they would build me a Drascombe Lugger, a craft which I thought admirably suitable for the Australian voyage. The Drascombe Lugger is an eighteen-foot day boat built along the lines of the traditional North Sea coble, a fishing boat used for many years in the cruel waters off our north-eastern coast. Within a few days I had a reply, inviting me to go down there. Mr Nicholls would be delighted to discuss any modifications I might require. In the early part of September 1968, I drove down to Devon, met him, and we walked over together to a half completed lugger.

'I would like the fore deck raised to the gunwale, with a three-inch crop, and a watertight bulkhead inserted,' I said while he scribbled busily in his notebook. 'I would also like a watertight bulkhead aft with two watertight hatches on the stern deck leading into the compartment. The stem head fitting I'd like to be made to take twin forestays, rather than the roller reefing gear for the jib. The frames will have to be cut back to allow for more living accommodation and the outboard mounting at the stern will have to be strengthened to take a larger motor.'

We walked down to the water's edge, where a pretty, bright blue Drascombe Lugger lay bobbing at her mooring. She looked desperately small. Nothing was said, but I could sense that Mr Nicholls thought that I was totally mad to contemplate such a voyage in a boat as small as this. Two varnished stubby masts swayed across the sky as she was hit by the wash of a small motor launch passing close by. I tried to imagine what this little craft would look like in the middle of the Indian Ocean.

I drove back to Emsworth that evening, deep in thought. I wanted to leave England in eight months. But my total financial resources were represented by the cheque that I had just received for *Atlantis*. Out of this I owed my bank manager £300, and so I had just enough to buy the Drascombe Lugger and her sails. I had no money for any equipment, so I started writing to manufacturers of yachting equipment, asking for help. I contacted numerous people, such as Wilfred Thesiger, who had been to some of the places where I was going and arranged to meet them: I was determined to gain every scrap of information possible on every part of the world I was likely to visit.

I spent days at the Royal Geographical Society library, poring over old maps and books and taking reams of notes. The vital necessity of correct timing for certain parts of the route was becoming clearer: I ought to be through the Aegean by the middle of July, before the meltemi wind began; and the Tigris would begin to get shallow in August, drying up very considerably in September and October, so I must be there as early as possible. In the Persian Gulf, the shamals, strong northerly winds, start in October, and I wanted to use the north-east monsoon in the Arabian Sea and the Bay of Bengal. So I made detailed plans, trying to take all these things into account. Any spare time I had was spent making up an endless list of all the equipment that I should take: food, radio transmitter, outboard engine, navigation equipment, charts, clothing, safety equipment, rope, blocks, tools, and so on.

On 1 January 1969 my little cockleshell was launched and named *Hermes*. I had found a crew member by advertising in The Times personal column—a complication was that he must be a film cameraman, because of the television contract I had. John Bennett joined me as soon as *Hermes* was ready for sailing. Trials began on 4 January, not the most suitable time of year for conditioning ourselves to the tropical weather ahead, but we had to make the best of a bad job. Our first task every morning was to knock sheets of ice from our canopy and to sprinkle salt over the fore and after decks. After the previous night's frost the sails would crackle with frozen stiffness and the sheets would be as hard as steel. After four hours on watch our hair would frost up, and often jangle with ice droplets. We always carried a life raft; the sea temperature was so low that if we capsized—which fortunately never happened—we would have begun to lose consciousness after only 20 minutes of submersion. Death would have followed 10 minutes later. To offset these discomforts, we at least had the sea completely to ourselves. The harbour was empty and the stillness and beauty of an early winter's morning was a memorable experience.

After each trial voyage, *Hermes* would be hauled out and brought into the carport of our house, where I would make any necessary modifications. The sheeting arrangements for the main and jib were positioned so that the helmsman could handle both with ease. I designed a canopy that would fit over the whole of the cockpit, to help protect us against the elements. But John was finding these trial voyages very trying; most of the time he was seasick and he was badly affected by the cold. But he plodded gallantly on without a word of complaint.

Slowly the various pieces of equipment began to arrive at my home. Much of it was on credit, some were gifts, and a few I had bought. By February my overdraft had begun to mount at the bank. Various potential sponsors began to show considerable interest in backing the project, but sadly many of these let me down, one by one. I had considerable help from some quarters, though—Messrs Heinz and Nestlé gave me supplies of tinned and dehydrated food, and Blacks of Greenock and Offshore of

Salcombe generously provided clothing and oilskins. The London Silk Centre became interested in the fact that part of our route would coincide with the old silk trading route, and presented us with a couple of silk dressing gowns to use as gifts to notabilities. The British forces stationed on the Persian Gulf were warned of my possible arrival and were asked by their London PROs to help me all they could—most helpfully, the RAF arranged to ferry some of my supplies to Bahrain. Yet, as the weeks drew on, the various problems increased in number and size until I thought that this voyage would never come off.

In early April—three weeks before I was due to set off—John telephoned me late one evening. 'I don't quite know how to put this,' he said hesitantly, 'but I'm afraid I think it would be best if I didn't come. As you know I've been seasick throughout most of the trials. I haven't picked up the knack of sailing as fast as I hoped, so I think I'd be more of a hindrance to you than a help.'

This was a nasty shock. It was a while before I found my voice. 'O.K., John, I understand. I'm just sorry it had to turn out this way.'

'I'm sorry about this too, Dave. I just hope you'll find someone to take my place.'

I put the phone down, wondering what to do next. I couldn't bring myself to be angry. John was thinking of the voyage and how it might fail if he came as crew. But the fact remained that I was left in a desperate situation.

The previous November I had interviewed one other person who had answered the advertisement in The Times Personal Column, a free-lance sound recordist. I immediately put a call through to him. 'Dave Derrick?'

'Speaking.'

'Oh, this is Dave Pyle. About this dinghy voyage to Australia. My crew member has backed out at the last minute. I know it's very short notice. But can you come?'

'Sure. I'll come.' Without any hesitation. Just like that.

'Splendid. Be in touch again tomorrow.'

My relief was tremendous. I knew virtually nothing about him, his capabilities, let alone his temperament. I was frankly apprehensive as to whether we would be compatible. But he would come.

The most heartbreaking event, throughout these long and difficult preparations, was the death of my mother in the first week of April. She had been admitted into hospital earlier in the year, slowly dying of cancer; throughout the first few months, I had watched her become progressively weaker. She knew that she was going to die, even though we tried to keep the truth from her, and showed tremendous bravery and courage throughout those last months. I felt that if just a small fraction of her courage could be brushed off on to me, I could come through any of the hardships that might confront me in the future. The feeling of sadness and loss was still with me, when, on the morning of 26 April, *Hermes*, David and I were ready to leave. It was a cold grey day, with a fine drizzle sweeping across the waters of Chichester harbour. My sailing club arranged a champagne breakfast and a small club gathering to see us off. Television crews, newspaper reporters and photographers came down in force, asking numerous questions and clicking away with their cameras. I was apprehensive over leaving on that particular day, at that particular time, as the weather looked doubtful; after a while I found I could not face all the ballyhoo, so I walked out of the club while the small party was still in full swing, and walked slowly down to *Hermes*, lying off the sailing club slipway. Eventually the crowd, with Dave amongst them, came down to the slipway as well.

Sir Alec Rose, and one or two of my old friends, shook us both by the hand and wished us good luck. My father was out on his boat and was planning to accompany us until we were just outside Chichester harbour. We climbed aboard, waved a farewell to everyone and sailed out to the club starting platform, where the starting gun was to be fired at the final send-off. At 10 am the loud bang echoed around the harbour—we were off.

We sailed our way slowly down towards the harbour entrance and the English Channel. With little warning a tremendous gust of wind whipped up the surface of the harbour to a frothy cauldron, and a torrential downpour of rain stung our faces. A sudden gale had set in from the south-west, without any warning from the Meteorological Office. I had no option but to turn *Hermes* around and sail towards the Royal Air Force Yacht Club on Thorney Island, a quiet corner of Chichester harbour, where we sat and waited for the gale to abate. My father came round to pick us up. The gale blew for a full twelve hours and that evening we had the doubtful privilege of watching ourselves leave on television! It was all a total anticlimax.

Sitting by the fire, we saw and heard Sir Alec Rose, who was asked by the interviewer to give his opinion on our voyage. He pinpointed one of my own major worries. 'I think their voyage is possible,' he said, 'but their main problem will be to stay together as a good, friendly, working crew. Sailing together in such a small boat, always in close contact with one another, under difficult and uncomfortable conditions, is going to be a great strain on them both. They may well find that they are totally incompatible, which would be the end of the voyage.' I didn't like to look across the room at the short, squat figure of Dave Derrick.

Late the following afternoon, 27 April, the weather had improved considerably; the seas had abated and the wind was blowing gently from the north. This time our departure was very different. There was just my father and my girlfriend, Julia, and we talked quietly, waiting for the moment to come when we would have to say our farewells once more. At six o'clock that evening, the shipping forecast sounded very favourable, and so I said goodbye to my father. He could not hide the anxiety from his face; he had just lost a wonderful wife and obviously realised that he might possibly be losing a son. For the second time in our lives, we shook hands and he quietly wished me good luck. Dave went for'ard and hoisted the sails. They slowly filled with the northerly wind and we slipped quietly out of the harbour into the English Channel, bound for Australia.

Hermes before painting, newly built from Kelly and Hall

Fitting out *Hermes*

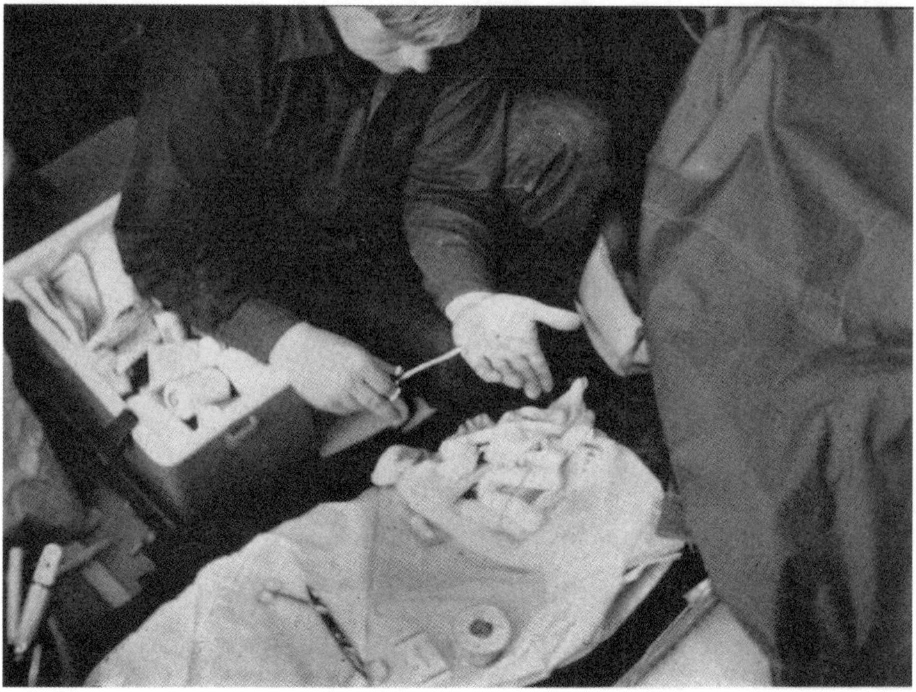

Extracting five stitches from Dave's hand in Paris,
after he had cut it badly on the tin foil from a film case

Loading up stores at Langstone

4

THE FIRST DAY OUT ON A VOYAGE IS ALWAYS A TAXING TIME for the skipper's nerves. As we settled down to the night crossing of the English Channel, I was very conscious of how little I knew of the other Dave, of how little I had seen of him as a sailor. My mind was also tormented with the thought that I had forgotten something desperately important. More worrying still was the thought that many in England undoubtedly thought that my voyage was impossible and would be half-expecting news of an early disaster. It was therefore of paramount importance that we should accomplish this 100-mile crossing of the Channel to Le Havre without mishap. From Le Havre we would go through the French canal system to the Mediterranean, so this first leg would be the trickiest bit for some time.

As I sat outside the small canvas awning, our only protection from the rain, wind and seas, my thought turned to the sordid question of money. I had £300 of my own money for the running costs of the voyage. Dave had put up the same amount, a total of £600 to last us a year, travelling a distance of nearly 13,000 miles. Up to the time of setting off I had already paid out close on £1000 and owed various companies another £500. My bank manager was willing to allow me an over-draft to see the voyage through, but only up to £300. This obviously meant that the voyage was being done on a shoe-string; we were going to have to be extremely careful with our running costs. We had been allowed to transfer, through the Bank of England, £300 outside the sterling area. We had to make this last until we reached Kuwait.

The night was crystal clear, with a slight swell running in from the south-west, the aftermath of the previous day's gale. The wind was blowing at a steady ten knots from the north and *Hermes* ran steadily before it, her twin genoas gently straining at their sheets. The thin wake streaming back from her bows caused a series of small wavelets to lap against the clinker hull. The weather was perfect. Yet I still felt uneasy. I lit the Primus stove, our only means of cooking, and filled the kettle from a polythene water-bottle.

The pink and blue flame licked around the base of the kettle, bringing a little warmth into the cold night air. Five minutes later Dave and I were both sitting with large mugs of steaming hot tea clasped in our gloved hands. We talked for a while as we watched the lights of the coasters and ocean-going cargo ships sailing up the Channel towards Holland, Germany and the Baltic. 'Roll on the Mediterranean. Let's have the warmth and sunshine,' said Dave, shivering in spite of three sweaters, two pairs of trousers and an oilskin. I, too, began to day-dream of the Far East islands, the palm trees, white sandy beaches and blue clear waters.

Such thoughts were quickly shattered when I radioed back to Niton, the GPO station on the Isle of Wight, requesting a message to be sent to my father telling him of our arrival two miles off Le Havre. On hearing of our intended destination, the duty radio officer made his opinion of our voyage only too clear. 'Good God, you must be mad,' he said. I thanked him politely, cursing quietly under my breath. I had spent months preparing for this, gathering all the equipment that I thought was essential, gathering every scrap of information to find out whether it would be feasible or not. I was certain that it was; yet here was a man who knew nothing of this condemning us out of hand. My determination to see the project through rose to new heights, and never dropped from that moment on.

Le Havre, guardian of La Seine, appeared on the horizon as a fortification built from the towering jibs of cranes and tall dirty industrial chimneys. Its harbour was covered with a thick film of black sludge-like oil, a sight sufficient to repel any unwary sailor. An intricate network of docks, basins and canals, enough to tax the nerves of the finest navigator, left us in some doubt as to how we were to continue southwards. We spent our short stay in the harbour readjusting *Hermes* and ourselves for the 900 miles of river and canal work that lay ahead. We decided to lower the masts from the beginning and went to work re-arranging the twenty-four square feet of our living accommodation (the size of a small dining-room table) for the coming month's voyage through France.

This task became all the more difficult after we had collected over four hundredweight of tinned foodstuffs from a shipping agent in Le Havre; the tins had been shipped across to save us the embarrassment of being overloaded for the Channel crossing. These tins were to be used on the waterways, so that we could conserve our dehydrated food. Actually it is no mean task for two men to eat four hundredweight of food in a month; in fact it is impossible, even with my appetite. We discovered this rather too late. Eventually I convinced Dave that he would suffer from claustrophobia if he slept low in the bilge, between the centreboard casing and lower planking, so he courageously volunteered to stow these cases of food on 'his' side, i.e. starboard, and to make his bunk on top of them. All cooking had to be done on 'my' side, port, with the air bed rolled forward; cooking on the after deck was out of the question, as fifteen gallons of petrol were lashed around the gunwale, and more below in the after lockers. But with a sheet of plywood on top of the watertight box containing the radio receiver and transmitter, we had a first-class dining-cum-chart table.

A side bench, a foot wide, ran around the cockpit area, nine inches down from the gunwale. The forward half of this contained a locker on either side, the port one having provisions for a week and the starboard one navigational equipment: radio, direction-finding loop, compass, dividers, parallel rule, pencils, current charts and Admiralty pilot guides. Under the rear half of the bench were two water tanks, port and starboard, holding 14 gallons each. For'ard of these were two heavy polythene watertight tubes, again on both port and starboard sides, with provisions in three and a chart in the fourth. Every inch of spare space was taken up with some item of equipment.

I had decided, many months before, that by far the quickest and surest way of reaching the Mediterranean was by using these French waterways. France offers a variety of river and canal systems, enabling the boating enthusiast to explore her most inland areas. From Paris on the Seine to Lyon on the Saône and Rhône, the main rivers running from the north and south of France respectively, there is a choice of three connecting waterway systems, enabling a yachtsman from northern European waters to travel down to the Mediterranean without getting his feet wet in the Bay of Biscay. Of the three systems, I had chosen Le Bourbonnais, almost equal to La Bourgogne in distance (642 kilometres) but having only 166 locks to the other's 228.

It was now 30 April; we awoke to a cold, drizzly morning all set to start on our first section, the Tancarville Canal running from Le Havre and leading into the Seine ten kilometres southwards. All went well until the final lock, which we found was not due to open for another six hours, when the flood began on the Seine. Fortunately it had turned into a beautiful day, with the sun shining down from clear blue skies. Without expending too much energy, we waited outside a bistro.

Eventually the lock gates were opened, whereupon the lock disgorged an odd assortment of barges. The skippers drove hell for leather up the Seine on the new flood, out into the wide world at last. These in turn joined forces with the larger coasters, ocean-going cargo-ships and 'pusher' barges, powerful blunt-nosed tugs coupled behind three 100-foot barges, all frantic to keep the flood under them, while little *Hermes* tossed and turned in their wakes, bravely puttering up behind. We felt infinitesimally small as these large, black steel hulks sped past, their engines rumbling, their large propellers churning the water into a crescendo of froth and foam around their sterns. Tides and currents play a large part in determining speed along this stretch. With a favourable tide behind us of two to four knots, six hours of motoring followed by six hours resting, we made good time to Rouen, travelling by night as well as by day.

At night my main worry was of our being run down by some large cargo-ship. We had mounted a small all-round white light on our mizzen mast, but since we were in confined waters it was up to us to keep out of the way of shipping. Since I knew very little of the other Dave's ability to negotiate restricted waters by day, let alone by night, and of his knowledge of navigation and lights, I took the helm throughout the night watches. These long periods of motoring were extremely monotonous, with the steady drone of the engine making it impossible to rest, even to think straight; I began to long for the day when we would reach the Mediterranean and hoist our sails once more.

I was surprised at how difficult it proved to navigate on this river, not so much from the fear of running aground but simply of knowing one's position. There is a form of pilot guide, but this is a little outdated, and our method of ticking off the bridges and locks to know how far we had gone became a mockery when we noticed new bridges had been constructed and old ones demolished. We eventually found that the easiest way, if in doubt, was to go close into the bank and read the road signs. This was a rather different form of navigation to reading a compass, sextant and chart, but it was the only method possible under the circumstances.

Rouen is the limit of tidal effect; south of this ancient cathedral city, we had to plug continuously against a head current of four or five knots. Due to heavy rains in the interior the Seine was in full flood. Since our best top speed, checked at regular intervals by my Walker log trailing over the stern, was only six knots, progress was slow.

We were having considerable problems with our cooking arrangements in these early days. When cooking, the port side was taken up with stove and cooking utensils, and from midships aft on the starboard side with helmsman and the rest with the cook. Underneath both helmsman and cook lay the food; somehow it had to be extracted from the cases. For our first few meals it was a question of pot luck; until we learned what case was where, we ate our way as cheerfully as possible through tinned rice pudding, followed by baked beans with a dessert of mushroom soup, or, if lucky, macaroni cheese. We overcame this by clearing out one of the side lockers and adopting a method I had used in previous voyages, of filling this locker with a week's supply of assorted food, and an occasional bottle of cheap vin ordinaire.

As we approached Paris we noticed the water changing colour rapidly from an acceptable greeny-grey to a dark brown, while the hills and countryside gave way to flats and factories. No longer were there quiet earth banks to lie alongside at night, but hard, rough, concrete walls. Barge traffic was also on the increase, and *Hermes* battered, tossed and twisted her way through the incessantly choppy waters. Bridges became a more regular sight with the Seine surging around their arches, making our progress even more difficult.

The start of the canal section lay to the south of Paris, only a day's motoring away, past a fully industrialised stretch of the Seine. The barges continued to surge to and fro, some more successful at their business than others, to judge from the private vehicles they carried on their decks; where normally a dinghy would sit, we saw anything from a bicycle to a brand-new Citroën. This was not only their work, passed down from generation to generation, but their home, their only home, and the women took a certain pride in their barges, forever scrubbing, cleaning and painting, or rearranging a bunch of flowers (using a spare propeller as a vase). We saw one barge in particular, heavily laden and with decks awash; but the woman still kept throwing her buckets of water and scrubbing vigorously, even though the river was swirling around her legs. Never have I seen craft so spotlessly clean; their cargo was often of coal yet the steel decks shone like mirrors, without a speck of dust or dirt to be seen anywhere.

The tempo changed abruptly when we entered the Canal du Loing, at the small village of Champagne-sur-Seine. Suddenly we were deep in the heart of the French countryside; the footpaths alongside the canal were still in good repair, and we didn't have to wait long before we saw our first horse-drawn barge. The wife was on the helm and the husband was leading his massive working horse at the end of the tow a hundred yards ahead. These barges not only have to accommodate the family but horses as well; a stable was rigged up just aft of amidships. Unfortunately they are a rarity now, and we saw comparatively few; the time is not far away when they will disappear for ever.

At the end of our first day, after negotiating sixteen locks and travelling forty-four kilometres, we reached a village so small that we could find no name to it. It had a small church, three old houses and a quiet little bistro. We left *Hermes* moored to the canal bank and walked to the bistro. The interior was simple and bare, the walls plastered with whitewash, with patches flaking away to show a mixture of sandy mortar and horsehair beneath. A few bare, scrubbed wooden tables were scattered over a well-worn red-tiled floor. At one of the tables in a far corner, where an oil lamp hung from the ceiling directly above, sat three bereted red-faced Frenchmen and a portly priest clothed in an old, well-stained soutane, playing cards. The air was strong with the smell of Gauloises and cheap red wine. They ignored us, as we sat at one of the tables and ordered a litre of vin ordinaire, a hunk of bread and some strong goat's cheese. We sat silently, savouring this pleasant, peaceful atmosphere.

So far the voyage had posed few problems. Life was running smoothly on board; Dave, although lacking in sailing experience, was turning out to be a first-class companion, quiet and reserved in his manner, but always a willing worker, and it looked as though we were going to make a very strong and compatible team. It had become a pastime of ours to rate and name the massive variety of French loos. *Hermes* lacked this particular refinement, which never bothered us at sea as we had a perfectly good transom, but on land we stopped regularly for this purpose. We soon discovered that the farther we penetrated into the French countryside the cruder their loos became. Indeed it seemed to us that the system hadn't changed over the last few centuries. Many of them were not only very dirty but needed gymnastic abilities to operate, with a two-foot-square cubicle, walls as smooth as glass and a nine-inch diameter bottomless hole in its centre. More than once I came very close to having a nasty accident.

Slowly the locks were ticked off. The Canal du Loing ran into the Canal de Briare and gradually we rose towards the summit at an altitude of over 600 feet above sea level. As we approached a lock one of us would drop off to help the keeper. Because of *Hermes'* size, only one gate would be opened; for the same reason the keepers were wary of flooding at any great speed. We were less wary, and would run around opening up all the flood gates at full bore. Whereupon the keeper would walk off, shrugging his shoulders, muttering darkly about 'the mad English'.

After the Canal Latéral à la Loire we began our descent towards the River Saône on the Canal du Centre. Here we met a series of automatic locks which proved even greater fun to operate. The gates open and close by the craft cutting the beam of a photoelectric cell. Once inside, with the gates firmly closed fore and aft, you are confronted with a choice of two coloured cords, blue and red. By pulling on one or the other, the lock will automatically empty or fill. When we met the first of these, an old, one-armed Frenchman came out of his hut and proceeded to explain at great length how the system worked. After finishing his lecture, he must have seen the blank expressions on our faces. 'Rouge descendant, bleu debout,' he said, shrugging his shoulders, he turned about and walked back into his little hut. I got the impression he did not really care if we wrecked the system, which is bound to make him redundant one day.

When we finally reached the Saône, with the promise of a continuous downhill run towards the Mediterranean, we were hoping to gain on some lost time, apart from the exciting prospect of shooting the sixteen-knot rapids mentioned in our pilot guide. To date the voyage had taken us nearly three weeks; I had hoped to complete the French waterways within this time. I was beginning to worry about the Tigris, over two and a half thousand miles away, our only passage from the Mediterranean to the Persian Gulf; as the summer progressed, it was slowly drying up in the fierce midsummer temperatures of central Iraq.

There was little we could do except to press on regardless. We motored down to Lyon passing into another famous section of the wine districts of France, producing two of the genuine red Burgundies from the vineyards of the Saône et Loire and the Rhône department. For this final section our pilot guide was really outdated. New hydro-electric schemes were sprouting up at regular intervals along the river; with their barrages, they reduced a previously torrential flow of water down to a sedate stream. Nowhere were we experiencing more than a four-to-five-knot speed in the river's current. The locks were vast in size and frighteningly deep, with *Hermes* a mere speck of flotsam in their depths.

At Le Donzère we were confronted with the deepest lock in the world, with a rise and fall of eighty-five feet, and our first spot of trouble with the law into the bargain. An announcement came from a loudspeaker by the lock entrance for us not to enter. We waited outside, while a strong cold wind blew from the north, blowing the surface of the river into a short deep chop which slopped over the gunwale. After a while a police van arrived and a gendarme called to us, pointing to a small jetty. Once alongside he jumped on board without a word and began to rummage in the lockers.

'What the hell's this?' I demanded indignantly. Still without a word he jumped back on to the jetty, beckoning with his hand for us to follow.

The three of us walked to the black Citroën van where a second gendarme was sitting at a radio set. Our friend said something, whereupon his companion began to send out a radio message. In my very bad French, I asked why we were being held.

'A woman in Chalon-sur-Saône says that you two stole her radio set from a café there.'

'But that's bloody ridiculous,' I replied. 'When did she report this?'

'This morning,' he said.

'But we left Chalon-sur-Saône three days ago,' I said, holding up three fingers.

This eventually proved our innocence, but it took from eleven o'clock in the morning, when we were first stopped, until five o'clock that afternoon, for the French police to give us permission to leave.

Soon we would reach the sparkling blue waters of the Mediterranean, able once more to hoist our masts and sails, with the peace of the untaxed, inexpensive wind to propel us. The outboard was serving us well, but the cost of running it had already mounted to about £100. *Hermes* would need a good sorting out before venturing under sail again, on the next leg of our voyage, the 2500 miles from Marseille to Mersin in southern Turkey. So rather than sailing out into the Mediterranean down the last of the Rhône, known as le Bas Rhône, I decided to cut off a section using a short canal system, and to spend a day in Port Saint-Louis, to prepare and store our equipment properly for sea-sailing.

When we were ready to depart, it began to blow hard from the south. But the short ten-mile hop across the Golfe de Fos to Port de Bouc was an enjoyable sail, and by the following morning the wind had died to a light westerly. We sailed the last thirty miles to Marseille in weather that one would expect of the Mediterranean, with the sun shining on the clear blue waters and the temperatures in the high seventies.

5

O N 23 MAY, AT THREE O'CLOCK IN THE AFTERNOON, we moored along-side a very expensive ninety-foot ketch, close to the harbour wall of Marseille. Dave and I immediately began to unload the boxes of tinned macaroni cheese, rice pudding, beans, mixed grill and chicken supreme, and to stack the tins along the top of the harbour wall. I then took a piece of cardboard and wrote *Pour Vendre* on it. Various Frenchmen came along, looked at the nasty tins, and shook their heads. Alas, no one seemed in-terested. Our immediate neighbours on their expensive gin-palace looked down upon us with unconcealed disdain.

My hands were tied. Somehow I had to dispose of the tinned food. It would be dangerous to sail through the Mediterranean with its bulk and weight; furthermore I hoped that a sale, although illegal, would ease our financial predicament. At sunset, I sadly took the notice down and left the tins on the harbour wall for anyone to help themselves. As I settled down for the night, I felt guilty at leaving them in this sad state, especially as they had been a gift.

Our financial embarrassment was already restricting our movements to an uncomfortable degree. We had adequate supplies of dehydrated food; water was free, so we would not starve or die of thirst. But on a voyage like this, small morale-sustaining articles are also needed. Both of us liked our cigarettes and our glass of beer, but the best we could manage now was to sit in a café with one cup of black coffee between us.

We talked incessantly about Naples, where I had arranged for a small sum of money to be sent. But there was a gale blowing from the south out-side the harbour. We had to sit and wait patiently, watching the wealthy smoking their Gauloises and drinking wine while we gnawed our finger-nails.

'That is something else altogether...' I said to Dave, eyeing a gorgeous young lady in a bikini as she walked along the pavement past our table. Dave grunted and licked his lips. We both watched as, waggling her hind-quarters, she walked up the gangplank of a luxurious chrome-plated motor launch, where she was greeted by a young, suave type in brightly coloured shirt and Bermuda shorts.

'Bastard, lucky bastard,' Dave murmured as he drained the dregs of our coffee.

The following Monday, we awoke to find that there wasn't a cloud in sight in the clear warm morning air.

Exactly one calendar month after we had left England, we cast off on our next leg, the 160 miles to the island of Corsica. Outside Marseille harbour we found a moderate westerly blowing; with the promise of fair weather to come, prospects of a speedy passage to Naples were good and we sailed along the French Riviera in high spirits.

With the exception of the Channel crossing, this was the first night spent at sea in which Dave had taken a watch. I was still unsure of how he would make out. Apparently he had applied for many expeditions, but this was the first he had managed to join. I found it difficult to find out exactly why he wanted to make such a voyage. It seemed that he did not mind how he travelled, whether it was by car to India, or on a canoe down the River Amazon. He just wanted to do something. I sensed that he felt that time was passing him by without any personal achievement, and that he needed some kind of ambitious voyage or expedition, before he became too old, as a challenge. Perhaps he was trying to find out something about himself.

Once more I had little sleep. When I opened a bleary eye, I noticed that we were still off St Tropez with the wind now hardly ruffling the sea surface. But weather in this part of the world is always unpredictable; as the morning advanced, a breeze set in from the south-east and by mid-day was blowing at 25 knots, and increasing. I took over from Dave when *Hermes* began to ship the odd short sea over her gunwales. If we were to meet any bad weather, I felt that I would be more at ease if I was on the helm myself; if Dave was on the helm and something drastic occurred, like a capsize, I would probably never forgive him, which would be unfair.

A number of craft were streaming towards the shelter of Cannes har-

bour and I decided to do the same. Of all the places to be without money—
Cannes, one of the largest playgrounds for the rich on the French Riviera.
The harbour was crammed with floating gin-palaces; their gleaming paint
and varnish betrayed that the massive yachts had never put to sea. Carpeted gangplanks, complete with chrome safety rails, led down from their
transoms to the jetty; we observed that often a drawing of high-heeled
shoes with Interdit written below was placed at the head of the gangway.
On deck, sipping their extra dry Martinis or exotic long cool drinks half
full of foliage, women of all ages sat or reclined—some very attractive
in bikinis, others revoltingly fat and ugly in their Bermuda shorts. With
mixed feelings I managed to squeeze *Hermes* between two of these yachts,
where no other boat could fit. At least this would enable us to escape paying expensive harbour dues.

'I'd like to take this lot out to sea and watch them get bloody seasick,'
I said, as we strolled around the harbour. 'Look at the rigging of that
mast. The damn' thing would collapse as soon as they hoisted the sails. If
they've got any.'

We had to wait for a day and a half before the wind veered from south-
east to south-west. It was still blowing quite strongly but now in our favour.
It seems that in the Mediterranean a wind from the western quarter brings
unsettled weather with it in the way of squalls and thunderstorms. All
winds along the French and Italian coasts have their own characteristics
and local names; the north-westerly is the predominant wind in the Golfe
du Lion and often in the Gulf of Genoa, and is given the name *mistral* by
the French from the old term magistralis or masterful one, and *maestrale*
or *tramontana* by the Italians. The strong south-westerly that we were experiencing at this time is known by the Italians as the *libeccio,* which blows
up into the Gulf of Genoa but often stops short of Genoa itself.

Against the advice of the local fishermen, who warned us of its strong
tempestuous squalls, we used the libeccio for the next three days. We had
already survived one of its squalls, and I had found that *Hermes* could
manage; but on the first day out as we sailed along the coast past Nice,
Villefranche and Monaco, we were hit by a tremendous wind and downpour of rain, far worse than we had experienced to date. I headed *Hermes*

for Port di San Remo, our first port of call in Italy. The wind blew hard all that night and the following morning, but by the time we had cleared customs, after having to dig deep into our pockets for 600-lire harbour dues, it had died away to a mere whisper. By carrying on up the Gulf of Genoa we would possibly have been stuck at its head with a predominant strong south-easterly blowing, so we decided to set sail from San Remo across the Gulf to La Spezia, a passage of 100 miles, instead of making for Corsica.

An hour after setting out from Port di San Remo found us still only 200 yards from the harbour entrance. The wind had died completely; *Hermes* just lolled in the glassy swell. I was fishing around in the food locker for something tasty to eat when I came across a 100-lire piece. As a boy I had often thrown a penny into the sea for King Neptune to produce some wind, so decided to try my luck. Valued at about seven and a half new pence, I thought the 100 lire should keep us in wind for a day or so, but I had not reckoned on the low cost of living in Italy. Within an hour the libeccio began to settle in once more, and I sent Dave forward to hoist the twin genoas. With the two large foresails boomed out on either side of the main mast, *Hermes* began to sail along at a tremendous pace. Helming became a nightmare as I struggled to prevent her from broaching; there was no doubt that we ought to reduce sail. But I thought this wind would be short-lived and that we should make the best of it while we could. Those 100 lire certainly went a long way; for the rest of the afternoon and the whole of that night there was no respite, and by early the following morning La Spezia lighthouse appeared right on the bow. The 100-mile crossing had taken us only nineteen hours, at an average speed of five point three knots. By the time we were abeam of the lighthouse, old Neptune evidently thought we had had our money's worth, because the wind died completely.

For nearly a day we drifted around a few miles offshore. There was no point in using the little fuel we had left to motor into the nearest harbour, as we had no money to spend when we arrived; we thought it better to stay where we were, so that temptations would remain out of sight. Eventually a pleasant westerly breeze arrived and we set off once more towards Livorno, fifty miles down the coast. The breeze stayed with us, and we arrived early the following morning. Here temptation stared us in the face once more, as we gaped at people sitting in the cafés, smoking, drinking their wine or beer, and eating delicious pastries. It was too much. I marched into the nearest bank, to get the money transferred from Naples. Soon we were smoking once more, and with the help of rich sickly ice-cream and pastries, turning our stomachs into acid baths. After spending the entire morning in unashamed luxury, we were ready to depart once more.

The wind was still in the west and all looked fine for a good passage direct to Naples. Later that evening, however, dark thunderous clouds began to roll in from the west. Lightning flashed along the whole horizon and I looked sideways at the oncoming seas which were increasing in size and hitting *Hermes* beam on. It looked like another batch of foul, squally weather coming, but very much worse than before.

'Better go forward and change the genoa for the working jib and get the main down.' I had a nasty feeling that we were heading for trouble. The black clouds were rolling in fast, and the lightning was an amazing sight, with incessant flashes lighting up the sky to the west in a perpetual ghostly glow. We knew the wind would soon hit. The seas were now very short and steep, increasing all the time; *Hermes* was finding it difficult to ride them in her usual buoyant way.

Since we were both partially blinded by the lightning, the sea seemed pitch black, but somewhere out there we could hear a tremendous roar that was coming upon us fast. Before I could bring her bows up into the oncoming wave, it hit us as a solid black wall. The force of it threw me across the helm, while Dave, sheltering below the canopy, suddenly found himself waist-deep in water. We both simultaneously made a grab for buckets, plastic bowls, anything to scoop the water out of our half-sunken craft before another such wave could hit us. I automatically backed the jib and sheeted the mizzen tight to windward, to bring her bows up into the oncoming seas, in time to stop another sea coming onboard. I held her there, while Dave worked like a demon clearing out the water. After a quarter of an hour the bilge pump was slurping out the last of the 30 gallons of sea water in the bilge, and we were fully operational again.

I felt immensely relieved at having come through this bit of trouble

Sailing off out of Langstone Harbour

Sir Alec Rose sees us off

A harpooned swordfish in Italy

Loading up *Hermes* on a truck in Mersin ready for the overland section; the author is bare-chested on the lorry

without too much damage; it also boosted my confidence in Dave, seeing him cope so well with what could have been a disastrous situation.

The rain soon followed. At least a tremendous half-hour downpour flattened the seas, making them no longer a hazard. The lightning was now overhead and I cursed my forgetfulness in not disconnecting the aerial lead and dangling it over the side as an earth. A lightning strike on that aerial would mean the end of our transmitter and possibly us as well. Meantime *Hermes* looked a proper mess. Our sleeping bags were soaked, the transmitter was flooded, odds and ends were scattered about her bilge. Three miles to the south lay the industrial harbour of Piombino; after three hours of sailing we made the harbour at two o'clock in the morning, for an unscheduled stop to reorganise ourselves. After a few hours we were off once more.

Later the same morning the weather began to look doubtful to the south, with the sky turning a dark grey. Inexperienced as we were in recognising weather conditions in the Mediterranean, we suspected it was bad, especially when a fishing boat came full speed towards us bound for Piombino; as they passed, the fishermen shouted excitedly, pointing to this dark grey mass which was now moving fast to the north. We were not going back, that was for sure; but according to the pilot guide the nearest port was over fifteen miles to the south, except for a small, silted-up fishing harbour four miles away near Punta Ala. I decided that we would try this; in any case the headland would give shelter from all winds south and west.

Slowly the seas began to rise, but with no sign of wind. In a North Atlantic gale the wind will pick up over a period of hours; here it was going to hit us hard and fast. We were a mile off the entrance of this little harbour, and could see the masts of other craft moored behind the breakwater, when I noticed the sea to our south. It was a steaming, seething cauldron, the crests of waves whipped off in a spume of spray. Suddenly the wind was screaming at a full forty knots. All sails were down as we were making way with the outboard; but *Hermes* heeled to an alarming angle, weighed down by the force of this screaming wind. I altered course to get the headland between us and the open sea, but this put us temporarily beam on to the waves which began to break over the gunwale. Dave had to return to his old job of bailing. After an hour, sixty minutes that seemed an eternity, we were tying up alongside a small jetty when an American lady strolled up to greet us.

'Gee, I like your yellow raincoats,' she said, with a disarming smile.

I was now becoming really concerned over the delays. Two thousand miles ahead of us the Tigris was slowly drying out in its upper reaches as the summer progressed. According to the various surveys over the past fifty years, it would be un-navigable north of the Samarra barrage after the month of July, and now it was 5 June. After two days of biting my fingernails, the wind seemed to be improving, and so I contacted the radio station at Civitavecchia, eighty miles south of us, for a meteorological bulletin. 'Velly good, velly good,' came the reply, so off we set once more. For three and a half days the weather was good; two and a half wonderful days of sailing before a moderate north-westerly, followed by a day's motoring in a flat calm into Naples harbour, weaving our way through the US Mediterranean fleet.

We moored *Hermes* in a yacht marina by the main harbour breakwater, squeezed between two fifty-foot luxury cruisers. She obviously felt uneasy and a little out of place, suffering the indignities of cigar ash falling on her decks from above, plus the occasional glace cherry and slice of lemon. Meanwhile we wandered up the steep, narrow, cobbled streets north of the harbour, amongst tall, rickety, crumbling houses that bowed to one another with their roofs almost touching. The washing was strung like a massive cobweb high above our heads; the stall holders were singing their wares in operatic voices, while live octopuses and eels slithered across the cobblestones, having escaped from their tanks. Some live chickens were still in cages, while others were tied to the legs of stalls; many were just running freely amongst the crowd. Occasionally we heard high-pitched screaming, as two women argued. Sometimes the 'discussion' developed into a free-for-all, as they struck at each other with broom sticks, while the men tried to hold them back. On every street corner, the master tradesman of Italy, the ice-cream maker, let it be known that his mix was best.

At night the back streets of Naples present a different scene. The

American sailors on shore leave, their pillbox hats perched at a rakish angle, spark off beauty parades on every street corner. Children of all ages act as the pimps, anything for quick and easy money. When we returned to a bar we had visited earlier, beer had suddenly doubled in price; a previously innocent-looking door now burst open, emitting from the thick, smoke-filled air, the smells of beer and wine, and the sound of coarse laughter and bawdy language. We ordered two glasses of cheap red vinegary wine.

'Never seen anything quite like this before, have you?' I said to Dave, watching a prematurely aged girl, probably no older than eighteen, trying to fix a price with an American sailor.

'No. And Naples is supposed to be one of the centres of the Roman Catholic Church.' The sudden transformation was baffling, strange, completely out of place. Both of us felt somehow very sad.

We had to stay in Naples for five days, waiting for some money to come through from England. I had decided from the start never to carry more than a bare minimum with us, in case it was stolen, and had made arrangements with my bank to send money out to various major ports of call. While we waited in the scorching sunshine, with clear blue skies above, the local children often visited us, trying out their limited knowledge of English. 'Got a cigarette, Joe?' 'I'm so hungry.' I regret that we taught them a few more words, which they would yell as they ran around the marina. Our neighbours would then glower down at us from above. We always smiled back sweetly. 'It's terrible what children pick up nowadays, don't you think?'

One afternoon we both took off to the barbers for our first haircut of the voyage. What unashamed luxury it was to be pampered! We entered, dirty, unshaven and stinking of sweat, and left clean shaven, with well-groomed, neatly parted hair and smelling of apple blossom.

When we finally left Naples on 14 June, sailing across the Gulf of Naples towards Sorrento, we were now approaching the Messina Straits, famous in ancient Greek and Roman history for its whirlpools and strong eddies with the romantic local name *bastardi*. The notorious Charybdis still exists off the coast abreast of Torre Faro, but Scylla, off the village of the same name, is now very feeble due to an earthquake in 1783 which altered the local topography.

The fascination of sighting a whirlpool gave us the wandering urge while passing through the Messina Straits. A day and night stop at the village of Scylla turned out to be fruitless in looking for one of these whirlpools, but not wasted, as it proved to be the most attractive little township we were to visit in our Italian coastal section. In the narrowest part of the Straits the only sign of turbulent water was a thin band of small wavelets stretching across from the coast of Sicily to the Italian mainland.

A few miles ahead of us lay the industrial port and centre of southern Italy, Reggio di Calabria. During our second night ashore, we were walking back from the town centre towards *Hermes* when we noticed two police cars, a truck and a small crowd of onlookers gathered outside a bank. Out of curiosity we decided to investigate. Part of the outside wall had been blown open and the police were removing the safe onto the truck. We left Reggio early, very early the following morning for the Gulf of Taranto.

The sheer cliff-like coastline of Italy's toe was now gradually flattening out to wide expanses of sandy shores, and we arrived at Crotone on 21 June. For a week or so I had been pondering over the amount Dave was smelling, and thought it was about time he sweetened himself up somehow. When I remarked on this, I found that he had been thinking precisely the same about me. We concluded that it must be our sleeping bags and personal effects, and spent the following morning on a massive washing campaign. That night, lying on our air beds, the smell was noticeably stronger, and we decided the following morning to give *Hermes* a good scrub out.

It didn't take us long to find the answer. Lifting up the bilge boards, we were greeted by a sight that was enough to turn the stomach of the most hardened sailor. In the bilge we had stored the tins of self-heating malted milk and cocoa; through continuous rolling and pitching, the ends of these tins had rubbed together and worn away along their rims. The contents had seeped out and mixed together in the bilges, producing, after a few weeks, a thick black sickly smelling mess.

The gale that had been blowing from the north-east for three days was now slowly moderating; so on 29 June we set off across the Gulf of Taranto with still quite a brisk breeze, and *Hermes* ploughed her way on a hard beat towards Capo Santa Maria di Leuca at the heel of Italy. Eighteen hours later in a flat calm, we motored our way into the little fishing harbour, our last port of call in Italy. Early that evening we set sail across the Strait of Otranto.

As we approached Corfu, a school of porpoises accompanied us, diving and swooping under our keel. A light westerly wind came across the smooth still waters, gently ruffling the surface. The temptation to stop for a while in one of the coves was almost irresistible. But time was against us, denying us the opportunity to indulge in romance. The following breeze was too good to miss; with twin genoas set, we sailed down her southern shores. By afternoon it was blowing a fresh twenty knots, and by early evening we were sailing down the mainland of Greece towards Preveza, one of the main harbours on her western shores. At one o'clock the following morning, *Hermes* was tucked snugly behind a breakwater in her third foreign country.

We badly wanted to escape being caught in the meltemi, a strong northerly wind blowing a continuous thirty knots, and often reaching gale force. This was due to start in the Aegean some time in mid-July, and would not abate until mid-September. It was now 2 July: we had under two weeks to complete a passage of over 400 miles, including a major stop at Athens. Although the wind was blowing strongly that afternoon from the west, we set off as soon as we could for the Corinth Canal and Athens. We only had to suffer two hours of unpleasant beam seas before we entered a short strait which came out into the entrance of the Gulf of Patros, between the mainland and the islands of Levkas, Ketallinia and Zakinthos. The following two days produced little in the way of wind, and we had a slow but pleasant passage through the Gulf of Corinth.

Before setting off through the spectacular Corinth Canal, we had to convince one of the officials that *Hermes* was capable of eight knots. This was the minimum speed allowed for any vessel passing through—easy enough for a liner, but for us virtually impossible. But we must have given an impressive display of her manoeuvrability, as we roared around the canal entrance, weaving in and out of buoys and boats, urging every ounce of speed from our outboard. If we could not manage eight knots it was likely that we would hold up the rest of the traffic.

In ancient times, long before the canal was built, thousands of slaves sweated and toiled, dragging the crude wooden ships over this narrow isthmus of land. For many thousands of years ships had to sail 300 miles around the south of Greece or be hauled overland. But on 6 August 1893 the first ship sailed from the Gulf of Corinth direct into the Aegean, through this four-mile man-made canyon, hewn from solid rock, a masterpiece of engineering. Sheer towering walls rise upwards 250 feet; as we passed through, we saw the marks of the foot and hand holds, where the men toiled up and down its precipitous face.

As we emerged at the other end, another official pounced on us, demanding canal dues. He was very pleasant over the whole affair, apologising over the amount it would cost us. We knew in advance that we would have to pay 600 drachmas, approximately £8.50, and were pleasantly surprised when he only demanded half this. A few hours after leaving the canal, we were motoring into Piraeus, the main harbour of Athens, on the hottest day of the voyage so far.

6

A S WE LAY ALONGSIDE A STONE JETTY, the sun beat down continuously from a translucent sky. The temperature soared into the mid-90s, without a breath of wind to stir our Greek courtesy flag. In such temperatures we were hardly in the mood for working, but I wanted the outboard motor to have a complete overhaul in readiness for what lay ahead.

To my knowledge, no European had navigated the entire length of the Tigris. Many would consider such a project an expedition in itself, but for us it represented only a part, a small part of the total voyage. In London I had gathered every scrap of information possible; but so little was known about its navigability, how many rapids we would encounter, and how bad they were, how many shallows. I began to fear that if anything was to wreck this voyage, it would be this section.

During the 1914-1918 war, British expeditionary forces had attempted to penetrate northwards into Mesopotamia from the Persian Gulf by using the Tigris; many men had died through cholera, malaria and the severe heat. The possibility of fatal disease made the thought even more terrifying. Our outboard was going to be the most important piece of equipment on board, our only means of power to help us survive the unknown hazards and difficulties. It had to be faultless, in perfect working order. Fortunately the Mercury agents in Athens were only too helpful, and gave the engine a complete service free of charge.

Our various chores were finished by 9 July, leaving us six days in which to complete the 300-mile Aegean crossing before the meltemi. We met a local fisherman mending his nets aboard his boat which lay close by *Hermes*. 'It always begins on 15 July,' he said. That same afternoon we hoisted our sails and drifted out of the marina. The light southerly breeze stayed with us throughout the night; it was a pleasure to be sailing once more. The skies were clear, studded with stars, and a full moon reflected itself in a shimmering ghostly white on the surface of the sea. Dark shapes of the rocky, mountainous islands of the Cyclades were littered all around.

The morning saw us off the island of Siros, whilst ahead, with their peaks rising above the horizon, lay Paros and Naxos. The Greek gods became famous with their wanderings through these beautiful islands. During his lengthy voyages throughout the Aegean, Ulysses often called upon these gods for help; like Ulysses, we were wandering in our little craft upon the same seas and through the same islands. We felt sad at having to pass by these enchanting islands, but with the etesian winds close at hand I felt that delay could be fatal.

By the afternoon we were sailing past the large bay on the north of Paros, with the idyllic little fishing village of Naoussa tucked away in one of its corners. The southerly wind began to increase in strength as we approached the island's north-eastern headland. Tufts of grey white clouds hung motionless over the mountain peaks, the tell-tale sign of a *sirocco*, a fierce hot southerly wind blowing off the deserts of Africa and Arabia. I was hoping to reach the port of Naxos, five miles east of us; we rounded the headland and after sailing only a few hundred yards realised the crossing would be impossible because a full gale was now blowing up the dividing channel of the two islands. We backtracked around the headland and attempted to make up to the head of the bay and Naoussa village. Here the situation was worse, with the wind blasting down from the mountain valleys; we were stuck on this rocky headland with only a small sandy cove for protection.

For two and a half days the sirocco blew. Once more I cursed the delay. Early on the third morning we were awoken by the crashing of thunder overhead and a brilliant display of lightning. The wind died almost immediately the storm had passed and by first light we were under way once more, sailing southwards between Paros and Naxos with a light northerly gently pushing us from behind. The following night we were weaving our way through smaller groups of uninhabited islands on a course for Amorgos. Daylight brought with it an increase in the wind, still from the north. It was now 14 July. The meltemi could have started a day early; rather than make our way along a rocky lee shore, with the possibility of another gale brewing, we headed into a narrow bay leading up to the village of Amorgos.

The local fishermen soon confirmed our suspicions. The etesian winds had begun and we had still sixty miles to go before Kos, an island off the south-western corner of Turkey. It was also the worst stretch if a northerly was blowing, with no protection from any islands except one, Levitha, which was very small and uninhabited except for the lighthouse keeper. For 300 miles north there was nothing, a long enough fetch for a northerly gale to produce a considerable sea. We had to take a chance and attempt the crossing now, before the seas really built up. We were faced with conditions that the normal dinghy-cruiser would shudder at the thought of sailing into, but we had been held up long enough. If we arrived at the Tigris too late, the voyage would be over. To sail across the rest of the Aegean, in conditions we knew to be dangerous for *Hermes*, was a risk we had to take.

The passage was choppy—the aftermath of the day's hard blow— but the wind stayed light until sunrise the following morning, when once more a stormy north-westerly began. Levitha was only half a mile off the bow; within half an hour we were sailing into a cove on her southern shore, the most perfect natural harbour in the Greek islands. We dropped anchor and both turned in for a fitful slumber on our now leaking air beds.

Later that morning we awoke to the noise of the wind howling through the rigging; *Hermes* was snugly settled in a well sheltered part of the cove, but we still had another forty miles of open seas to cross before we were out of danger from these winds.

For three days and three nights it blew a full gale. The first afternoon we explored the island, which, being so small, took us only a few hours. The following two days were spent fishing, our total catch being one dozen assorted gaily coloured fish, the largest only four inches long and all completely inedible. On the second day a large, 100-foot chromium-plated gin-palace came into our small sheltered harbour. Since it was flying the British ensign, we thought in our innocence that maybe they would invite us over and that we might spend a pleasant afternoon with them. When six of the occupants came ashore in a launch, landing close to where we were anchored, I gave them what I considered my friendly smile.

'Good afternoon,' I called out cheerfully. Two of them looked at me haughtily. Ignoring my greeting, they turned away and began walking inland.

'The stuck-up bastards,' said Dave in disgust. We retreated to the shade of the sun awning.

On the fourth day I decided that we had been on the island long enough. For a few hours the previous night the wind had moderated, and might do so again tonight. The seas, with the long open fetch northward, would be quite large, but forty miles to the east lay the island of Kos. Its harbour was a farther fifteen miles on its eastern extremity, but to its north lay Kalimnos, and a few other smaller islands, giving some kind of shelter. During the early part of the evening we stowed the perishable gear into polythene bags and watertight compartments. All movable objects were lashed down; our external buoyancy tanks were fixed around the gunwales but left deflated; by nightfall we were ready.

Maybe it was the urge to move again that made us think the wind had abated, or perhaps it actually had; anyway, with only the genoa up we crept out of our little cove. The odd squall burst down from the steep, hilly slopes, pushing *Hermes* out into the open sea. For a while all seemed well; the wind was from the north-west and Levitha offered some protection from the seas. But as we came out from under her protecting shores, it soon became evident that we had a rough passage in store. The seas were running in onto *Hermes'* quarter, and I kept glancing over my shoulder with a wary eye, estimating their size and potential danger. The seas were hitting *Hermes* ten to fifteen degrees off the stern, which was a minor consolation. At least this was preferable to a direct run, where she would career off on either tack while surfing down the front of the waves. But it meant a continuous strain in one direction on the helm, trying to prevent her rounding up into the seas and being hit beam on. It took all of my strength to keep her on course and the thin laminated tiller often bent at an alarming angle.

Within half an hour of leaving Levitha, the wind suddenly increased and the seas began to break and foam past us. 'Get the genoa down and change it for the working jib,' I yelled, trying to make myself heard over the roar of the seas and the screaming wind. Dave was now highly proficient at changing headsails, and the working jib made helming that little bit easier. Meantime my brain was working full-time, trying to work out what was the most practical solution to our problem. I thought of heaving to and lying to the sea anchor; but this would be completely impracticable, as the northern rocky shores of Kos were to leeward of us, and in time we would have been driven upon them. The only solution was to run before the wind and seek shelter farther on.

After an hour the wind subsided from a full gale to twenty-five knots. I was extremely tired, with racking pains in my arms that made it almost impossible for my hands to grasp the tiller, and so I handed over to Dave. Ten minutes later another squall hit us. I could sense that Dave was having difficulty in handling *Hermes*; although it was pitch dark, I could see that he was hauling erratically upon the helm. I could just make out a peculiar expression which I had never seen before, upon his face. His eyes were wide and staring, his mouth a hard thin line. He was frightened, as I was, but this was the first time I had seen him show any signs of emotion.

Suddenly a monstrous wave came up from the stern like a car on a big dipper, *Hermes* was picked up in a welter of foam and surfed down the face of the wave, skidded sharply to port and was then hit beam-on by a breaking crest. We both clambered frantically to windward, to try to keep her on an even keel. My mind was reeling. Certain that we were going over, I gasped for breath and swallowed a lungful of water. Coughing and spluttering, I instinctively grabbed the helm to try and bring her back on an even course. But when I caught hold of the thin, frail wooden stick, it fell to the bottom of the boat, broken off at the rudder stock.

We were crippled and helpless. Something had to be done quickly, for we were wallowing low in the water, slowly filling up as every wave came at us. Six successive walls of water smashed against her sides and gallons of sea water flowed into the bilge. Suddenly I remembered that the outboard was still connected. Reaching for the starting cord, I pulled, and it started first time. Slowly I brought her back on course; Dave began to bail frantically, while I sat right aft on the petrol tank trying desperately to prevent her broaching again.

But I soon found that at the top of each wave the propeller would not bite into the turbulent crests, and that she would begin to career wildly off course. I could do nothing to prevent her. But in the troughs the propeller would bite deep into the water, and I had to bring her quickly back on course before the next towering wave, the height of a two-storey house, came crashing upon us once more.

After ten nerve-racking minutes, I began to notice a strong smell of petrol. With my left hand I felt around under the engine cowling. Petrol was leaking profusely from somewhere in the engine, but this was no time to stop to find out where. Minutes later the outboard began to splutter and to cough and then died. Once more without steerage way, *Hermes* swung up to port and was filled by the following wave. So much for all Dave's hard work. I squeezed the hand pump, a little rubber valve on the fuel line, and tried again; at the first pull it burst into life, only to die away again ten seconds later. Squeeze, pull and away again; all I could do was to keep on pumping the fuel through slowly by hand.

Obviously the main petrol pump must have broken; all that was getting through to the carburettor was the trickle that I pumped by hand. The rest of our precious petrol was just flowing away. We did not have a vast supply of fuel and were only functional while the outboard ran. My hands were fully occupied, so Dave brought out the dripping, saturated chart, which was beginning to fall into little pieces, and shone the torch on it. I noticed that the small harbour of Kalimnos lay twenty miles from us; this was a good fifteen miles closer than Kos, but to the north-east. From our present position Kos was a lee shore and we were slowly being pushed upon it. Somehow we had to fight our way to seaward, towards Kalimnos—which would mean bringing *Hermes* round farther to port, to receive the seas on her beam. Which was exactly what we had been desperately trying to avoid.

I tried to steer as best I could with the motor, squeezing the fuel pump every five seconds and judging each wave as it came—whether to stay on course or run. Dave was continually bailing. As soon as he had partially cleared the bilge another wave would break onboard and his work would start all over again. Some of the waves could safely be negotiated beam on, but many others necessitated our turning tail and running before them. I kept peering ahead into the dark void of the night, searching for a small light that would indicate the harbour of Kalimnos.

For three hours I held to our course, numb with exhaustion, my mind whirling with the fear of capsizing. We were well equipped for survival if *Hermes* foundered and sank, but my fear was for the loss of the boat and all her equipment. My entire life savings and more had gone into this voyage, my hopes, dreams and years of planning. To end the voyage with *Hermes* a wreck was a prospect that I considered worse than death itself.

At last I caught a glimpse of a small flashing white light, which disappeared behind a wave. A line of rocks extend two miles off the southern shore of Kalimnos, and this light was on the southernmost one. For what seemed like hours there was no apparent change in our position. That little flashing jewel kept beckoning us to safety, yet seemed to get no closer until suddenly we caught sight of spumes of white spray and foam and heard a loud thundering roar. Slowly our eyes began to pick out dark jagged shapes of rocks; the light became clearer, gradually rising above us, and then moving fast along our port side. We felt a sudden exhilarating sense of speed as a large wave picked us up and swept us around behind this rocky chain. Immediately the seas decreased in size, having expended their tremendous force on the rocks to windward.

Dawn was breaking as we motored into the still waters of the harbour. Suddenly the physical exhaustion after the last eight hours hit us, and hit us hard. Dave tried his best to produce a hot, sweet mug of tea, but I wasn't interested. My clothes and sleeping bag were soaked, but when I lay down I felt as if I was in the most comfortable of dream beds with silken sheets. Although I was strangely exhilarated at having brought *Hermes* through, I just wanted to forget the last few hours.

Dave and I had been together now for over two and a half months. Despite Sir Alec Rose's prognostication, we had not fought, or even had a decent row, as yet. There had been minor disagreements, but always so trivial that within minutes all had been forgotten. I think that a mutual understanding of the inherent dangers contributed considerably to our compatibility. The storm which we had just been through tied us together, not so much in a bond of friendship, as by our need for mutual, moral support. Real friendship had not, indeed never, developed between us; our attitudes were too divergent, our personal ways of life too disparate for friendship to take root and flourish. Lack of patience was my biggest failing, together with an inability to accept other people's ideas. I realised from Dave's face that at times he found this irksome, but he would say nothing, and in turn I would find his long periods of silence disturbing. But we managed to put up with one another's peculiar ways and accepted each other's faults.

We slept until the heat of the day made further rest impossible. The meltemi was still blowing from the mountain slopes above us in short, hard gusts. But *Hermes* was in a shambles, and our first task was to clean up. My main concern was for the transmitter; although it was in a supposedly watertight box, water was seeping in from somewhere and so we had to strip it down and dry it out. The outboard needed repairing, which was relatively easy; the fuel pump diaphragm had perforated, but we had a spare and within half an hour all was well. Repairing the bracket for the tiller was fairly simple once we had found a blacksmith; to make sure that this could not occur again, we replaced the original cast bronze fixture with one of steel. As evening approached, *Hermes* was almost fully functional again. With the exception of fuel, we were ready for the next leg to a new country and for the overland section of the trip. With many islands now to the north of us, the seas were of only moderate size along the short passage to Devenboyria Point, the south-western tip of Turkey, and the Turkish mountains gave us a splendid sheltered 100-mile passage to Marmaris, our first port of call in Turkey.

7

Marmaris has a magnificent harbour; the steep, densely vegetated mountain slopes run down to the shoreline, fjord-like in character, so that this port could easily be on the Norwegian coast. As we approached the narrow entrance, we heard a continuous high-pitched whistle, increasing in volume until it was coming from all directions and almost deafened us: birds, thousands upon thousands of birds living in the forests on the mountain slopes were simultaneously bursting into song with ear-shattering results.

We moved alongside a jetty in the heart of the town; the health, immigration and customs officials were still in bed, and it was an hour before things began to move and a further six hours before it was all finished. Tramping from office to office, a stamp here and a stamp there, filling in reams of forms, but not knowing the reason, can be very demoralising. We ended up with six forms, all plastered with stamps: one was for health, one for immigration, one for customs, and three which to this day had unknown origins.

A light north-westerly took us out of Marmaris harbour bound for Mersin, the last stage of sea voyaging before the Persian Gulf. Ahead lay my biggest worry, the 500-mile overland section and a 1000-mile voyage down the Tigris to the Gulf. We were to experience one of the hottest regions of the world in as crude a form as the men in 1916: no air-conditioning, no fans, no ice-cold drinks, just the protection of a sun awning and a hat. Nor were we fresh from a base, well-fed and watered, but wearied after 3000 miles voyaging in an open boat.

The last of the money allowed to be transferred outside a sterling area, through my agreement with the Bank of England, was waiting for us at Mersin, 500 miles away. We had enough fuel for 100 miles, and I was hoping for land and sea breezes along this coast to keep us on the move. For the first two days it was more the current than the wind which drifted us a total of forty miles. Eventually we reached Antalya, a reasonable-sized township, 120 miles along the coast. Speed was now essential: after travelling only 3000 of the proposed 12,000 miles, we were already a month behind schedule. Every day the Tigris was becoming that little bit shallower, so our stay was limited. Fresh water, provisions and fuel were taken on board and we were ready once more to set sail.

No sooner had we set off than we were to regret taking on so much fuel. A moderate westerly began to blow and stayed with us for days. For the navigator, life along this coast can become a nightmare, especially when under the heading of 'caution no. 3' he finds that a particular headland is two miles farther south than charted. There are precious few navigation lights; by day we would sail close inshore, to gain the maximum benefit of the sea breezes, but at night, with the rocky cliffs and mountains taking on a dark and sinister look, we would automatically steer away from them—only to find ourselves, at first light, ten miles out to sea. It was along this coast that we heard the first moon landing described on the radio, and felt that we were more qualified than most to appreciate such an achievement. Even so, we could not quite banish from our minds a tinge of resentment: here we were, trying to achieve something on our own earth that had never been done before, at a cost of a few hundred pounds, whilst up there were these guys exploring a planet, at a cost of many hundred millions of pounds. Inevitably we asked ourselves: 'Is it worth it?'

At mid-day on 28 July, *Hermes* slipped in behind the large new concrete breakwater of Mersin harbour. To starboard, cranes were loading modern ocean-going cargo-ships, with large concrete office blocks and flats in the background. To one side of the main harbour I saw a small boat basin with a wooden jetty, and headed *Hermes* towards it.

Work now began to make the boat ready for the overland section. When I unshackled the shrouds of the mizzen mast and hauled it out, a gust of wind caught the mast, with radio aerial still attached. I lost my balance and the lot fell into the water—mast, aerial, Turkish and British ensigns. There was a yell of dismay from the shore and a uniformed young Turk ran down towards us, his face flushed with anger, pointing excitedly at the Turkish flag which had been unceremoniously dipped three feet under water. I tried to apologise and to make amends. I hauled the dripping flag out of the sea and hung it up to dry on a wooden rail. But it was one we had made ourselves by glueing bits of material together; his face began to drop and I thought he was even going to cry, as he watched the white quarter-moon and star slowly peeling off the dirty red square of cloth. For a moment he looked at us with fierce hatred, before turning on his heel in disgust and walking away.

Both of the masts were dropped and stowed, and all the loose gear packed up in polythene bags.

Visas for Iraq were waiting for us at the Iraqi Embassy in Ankara, but according to the Iraqi Embassy in London we both had to go and present ourselves in person before we could receive them. This meant that we would have to leave *Hermes* and all our belongings unprotected. Apart from Dave's camera, it wasn't the value in cash terms, so much as the total inconvenience of having anything stolen. At this point we met a young Turkish naval officer who had wandered over to see our boat and suggested that we should moor *Hermes* alongside the naval jetty, where we knew she would be safe. The following day we boarded the coach for Ankara very much easier in mind.

Ankara was 250 miles away in a north-westerly direction, almost the opposite direction from our intended destination. When we had collected a mass of mail from our friends and relatives back home, we called at the Iraqi Embassy for our visas, only to discover that we had left all our passport photographs on board *Hermes*. When we looked around, we realised that photograph slot machines have yet to arrive in Ankara. But the street photographer, with his wooden box-camera on a tripod, offers, through a crude but ingenious system, to produce a picture in ten minutes. His camera is simplicity itself, a wooden box about eighteen inches square and a lens with a cap fitted over it. To focus, the camera or subject is moved backwards or forwards. Inside that magic box are sheets of negative paper, developing fluid and all the tools of the trade, the first Instamatic ever invented.

I walked up and sat in the chair provided, which belonged to a neighbouring café. With professional concentration he moved my head around until it was in position; then, reaching forward, he took off the lens cap, counted five and replaced it. The mystery then began; under cover of a dark cloth, he half climbed into his box. Five minutes later, sweat pouring down his face, he produced a negative. This was placed on a special frame at the correct distance from the lens, the cap removed, another count of five, and the cap replaced once more. Diving back into the camera box he started work again. Another five-minute wait and, hey presto, my photograph: a refugee newly released after five years in a concentration camp.

Having travelled overnight back to Mersin, clutching our precious visas, we found *Hermes* safe and sound and spent the following day trying to find a truck and two drivers willing to take us the 500 miles to the village of Cizre on the River Tigris, on the borders of Turkey, Syria and Iraq. Many tales of bandits had been coming through from the mountains of the old Kurdistan area; since our route lay through these lands, with Cizre in the very heart, no driver was keen at first and the price had to be raised accordingly. Negotiations were eventually finalised, at 1000 Turkish pounds for *Hermes* and ourselves, food to be provided by the driver. £45 for a 500-mile journey is of course exceptionally cheap by western prices; but this was double the normal rate for such a distance, according to one of the naval officers in Mersin.

That same morning of Friday 1 August, the truck arrived with the owner and his mate, two dirty, half-shaven, bored-looking Turks. I was thankful that I had written a lengthy letter home giving full details of what was happening; we were about to enter unknown territory, and it was as well if someone knew, in as much detail as possible, our plans for this next stage. Twelve ratings of the Turkish navy were detailed to help us load the truck; within an hour *Hermes* plus three-quarters of a ton of equipment were on board and lashed down.

We made regular stops en route at small, grubby transport cafés. Most of them consisted of a small wood and corrugated iron shack, with a wood-fired stove. The food was always boiled mutton, and a few very hot peppers, which the Turks ate by the plateful, with a hard cake of unleavened bread and a slice of water melon for afters. We ate the same as our two drivers, but omitted the peppers. We also stopped frequently to pick up paying passengers, families of wandering Turks, Bedouin in character but without camels. They often seemed to be travelling hundreds of miles in search of work on the land, living in crude tents alongside the road, waiting hopefully for trucks to pass. For a small sum they would ride to some village a hundred or so miles farther on. At first I was a little huffed about them clambering on *Hermes*, but as time went on I began to change my tune. After 300 miles the tarmac road ran out, and we were left with dirt and stone beneath us. *Hermes* was thrown violently from side to side; but by piling the bodies onboard, this motion was lessened considerably.

On the second day we came into the mountain foot-hills and our two drivers began to cause trouble. They gave every excuse in the book why they could not go any farther: the road was too bad, the engine was playing up, they hadn't enough fuel. They pointed to the fuel tank and pointed to the engine, which steamed incessantly, shrugging their shoulders in a sign of hopeless despair. But we were now two very tenacious and rather desperate men, unwilling to stand for any nonsense. We finally came to an understanding that we would only travel through the mountains during daylight hours.

This satisfied them to some extent, and we drove on to Mardin, a nearby town, and stopped for the night.

The following morning we slowly ground our way up the steep dirt road into the Kurdish mountains. The sparse vegetation gave way to tufts of parched yellow grass, with grey, lifeless boulders scattered at random over the slopes. Rust-coloured sandstone cliffs hung precariously outwards above our heads. Behind us the view was lost in a single unending dust cloud billowing out from the truck's rear wheels, seeping through the cracks and holes in the floor beneath us.

After 200 miles of this barren mountainous wasteland, in temperatures of 110°F, with choking dust clogging our noses and drying our throats to the consistency of glass paper, we began to descend. Ahead we glimpsed, for the first time, the Tigris river, meandering through the valley below, an oasis of beauty with cool, swift-flowing water. The village of Cizre could be seen, a group of houses huddled around the river bank. From our vantage point we could also see two other countries, Syria and Iraq, spread out to the horizon, a barren and inhospitable sight giving us an idea of what lay ahead. Our driver celebrated by crashing into gear and stepping sharply on the accelerator, throwing us and our paying guests in a mass of arms and legs on top of *Hermes*. We were swayed and jolted with spine-breaking fierceness, as we descended the winding mountain track towards Cizre.

Within a short space of time we were at the main crossroads where a policeman stood on a box directing the traffic. Besides ourselves, there were four water-carrying donkeys and a man-powered cart on the one and only main street, which was largely blocked anyway by market stalls and farmers selling their fruit and vegetables. Filth, poverty and stench invaded our eyes and nostrils. A malodorous miasma hung in the air from the open street sewer and the unclean sweaty bodies of the villagers. Neither Dave nor I had ever encountered such a scene or such a smell before and we both felt a little sick.

Our two friends obviously felt uneasy. They had been driving for ten hours without a break, and showed no interest in food or refreshments. Without our consent, six labourers were recruited and driven, with *Hermes*, down to the river bank. Within an hour the boat and three-quarters of a ton of equipment had been off-loaded; by the time I had paid our helpers, who miraculously doubled in number the moment I pulled out my wallet, the truck was just a speck on the mountain-side followed by a cloud of dust; our two chauffeurs, plus four of our polythene water-bottles and the only map we possessed of this area, were already on their way back to Mersin. As we watched them go, we wondered at the reason for their desperate departure; when we turned round, we saw that some of the locals were already trying to pilfer our equipment.

An outsider, on seeing two Englishmen with a little yellow boat stuck in the middle of the Kurdistan mountains, might find the sight extremely hilarious. But for us it was a serious business. We were stranded in a hostile village, cut off from any outside help. Whilst I was wondering what to do next, two Syrian jets screamed overhead, reminding us that a war was being fought not so very far away. A mile downstream the Tigris became the no-man's-land between Turkey and Syria; the continual dispute over who owned the east or west bank or both would put us in a tricky position for the first twenty miles—before sailing into Iraq. As innocent voyagers we were now confronted with political disputes, and no amount of sailing skill would be of help to us here. There was only one solution: to take a British stance, with stiff upper lip. Our only hope lay in keeping calm and in not allowing the enemy to get excited.

Leaving Dave with the thankless task of protecting our boat and equipment from pilferers, I went off to see the police and customs for what I hoped, in true British style, would be 'peaceful' talks. Unfortunately my fluent sign language was incomprehensible and we spent a futile half hour with no satisfactory results. But the name of Hassan occasionally cropped up during our 'conversations'. Eventually one of the customs men was sent off to find him, to return ten minutes later with one of Ali Baba's forty thieves. Hassan was the village bilinguist, fluent in English obscenities with a spattering of the odd noun and verb. He explained that he had learned English while acting as a driver for the British forces in Iraq. With Hassan acting as interpreter, I soon gathered that the Turkish authorities were far from keen on letting us go down river, that a certain tension existed between the Turkish and Syrian troops, and that it was more than likely that we would be shot at from both sides. If we were lucky enough to escape injury on that section of the river, we certainly would not escape the Kurdish bandits in the north of Iraq. Dave and I were both well aware of these difficulties and I explained that the responsibility was ours. But no matter how much I pleaded our case, nothing would induce these boys to give us our clearance papers. Nothing. Finally, looking at Hassan, who gave a despairing shrug, I walked back to Dave.

'We're in a bit of trouble, mate,' I said, raising my hand at one of the children who was peering too curiously for comfort at our equipment inside *Hermes*. 'They're not giving us permission to go down river.'

'So what the hell do we do now?'

'To be quite honest I don't know,' I replied. 'We'll just have to sit down for a while and think this one out.'

Our position was now embarrassing, to say the least. Of course we could miss out on the Tigris altogether, go all the way back to the Mediterranean. 'We could sail around Africa,' I said cheerfully, 'but it would add at least a year to the voyage.' Dave looked glum. But if we adapted our current plan, I calculated that we would have to take ourselves by train to Mosul, a town on the Tigris in northern Iraq. That, however, would entail a train journey through Syria and the Syrians had made it only too clear to me at their Embassy in Paris that a visa was not granted to British or American subjects, even if only in transit. But Mosul was on the main Istanbul to Baghdad line. The nearest railway station on the line, from our present position, was at Nusaybin, on the Turkish/Syrian border. It was only 120 miles to the west of us. Worth a go.

'Let's have a bash at getting through Syria by train,' I said, after being silent for a full ten minutes.

'Doesn't seem to be any alternative. Worth a try, anyway,' Dave replied.

We discovered that a coach of sorts left every day from Cizre to Mardin, which was fifty miles west of Nusaybin. If some other means of transport could be found for the remainder of the journey, we could leave the boat at Cizre and go off to survey the possibilities of taking it by train first. I discussed this with Hassan, who found us a young lad to look after *Hermes* while we were gone, and invited us up to his home for a meal.

To add to our troubles, I was now showing all the symptoms of dysentery, and had spent the day making regular visits to the local hotel's commode. The prospect of more Arab and Turkish food was distressing, but the evening turned out to be very entertaining, and we learned a lot about the ways of these people and of Hassan's exploits. His home was originally a square, white-bricked bungalow, but because of his rapidly increasing family, both children and wives, another storey was being built on top. At the moment he had two wives and nine children, but a third wife had just been bought from a Kurdish village fifty miles to the east, and another room was being built to house her. His business was more obscure. He owned a three-ton truck which his brother drove between Turkey and Iraq, and occasionally into Syria, smuggling tea and tobacco. Sadly he explained that business was not so good, as the customs and police were asking for more money every time, leaving very little profit for him.

The coach took the same mountain roads, but was slightly more comfortable than before, with occasional stops for food and drink, which I used for other purposes. Early in the afternoon we jolted our way into Mardin. After wandering around the hot dusty streets for two hours we noticed a small courtyard with a very battered Chevrolet parked in a shady corner. The driver said that he would be leaving for Nusaybin in half an hour and would take us along.

Eight passengers were packed in like sardines, as the car rumbled along the dirt and stone road. Running along our right side lay a high barbed-wire fence, whilst 200 yards farther in lay another. In between was the no-man's-land. Notice boards carrying a red skull and crossbones were hung at fifty-yard intervals, and others with blood-red lettering labelled *Danger—Mines* told us the situation very clearly. The Syrian flag was flying from occasional concrete blockhouses dotted along the horizon. To our left there was another barbed-wire fence, with the Turkish flag flying from small mud and brick buildings. We passed the odd group of weary and dejected Turkish soldiers, dirty, unshaven, and totally exhausted from their futile guard duty. The scene depicted only too well the extreme seriousness of the situation that we were in. If we crossed the Syrian border uninvited, there was little chance of seeing our homeland again.

Later that evening, lights of a fairly large village began to flicker on the horizon, and in half an hour we were driving up the main street—a dirt road studded with potholes. We were dropped outside the only hotel in town, which looked surprisingly respectable compared to its neighbours. The proprietor seemed surprised to see us; when we enquired about travelling by train through Syria, he replied that he didn't see that they would stop us. Our situation was still tense, but at least we seemed to be making progress. The following morning we visited the railway station and were given the same news. I wondered if everything was not beginning to sound just too easy. The Turkish people have no trouble in crossing the border into Syria, and did not understand our difficulties in these parts, being British subjects. Whether we would ever get out of Syria again was another matter, but it was worth a try, visas or no visas.

I wanted to return to Cizre as soon as possible, to fix up another truck for the road journey. Already I had visions of the villagers kitted out in our clothing, with Hassan's boy unable to stop them. But nothing was travelling to Mardin that day. Eventually we found a truck leaving for a village on the Mardin-Cizre road, where we could pick up the coach returning to Cizre. The truck was travelling directly through the mountains to the north, along a rough mountain track where Europeans were advised not to venture; by this time we were as dirty and unshaven as any of the locals, and I considered that we blended in admirably. We joined the 40-odd peasants and their belongings on board. A mile out of Nusaybin the road petered out to nothing but boulder-strewn river beds, and open barren valleys winding their way down from the parched mountain slopes. The heat, stench and dust were unspeakable. Occasionally we would stop while a family with bundles of belongings would alight and wander off into the barren waste without a sign of habitation anywhere. Others would suddenly appear from behind boulders to take their place.

The journey dragged on into the scorching heat of the afternoon. We had come totally unprepared, and our mouths and throats were sore and parched. Our fellow passengers noticed our plight and offered us some of their water and their meagre supply of food. They tried so hard to communicate and to be friendly, talking to us in a mixture of sign language and Turkish. We were both deeply touched, and my feelings towards these people began to change. One old man, standing beside me, managed to tell me that an avalanche had occurred on this road, which smashed on to one of these trucks full of travelling peasants. He chattered away excitedly and at the same time told his story with his hands, as we passed beneath the towering overhanging cliff of loose sandstone rock. A few minutes later we passed through a small village, where a group of small children threw dirt and spat at us; the old man sent a flurry of scathing words at them and began to dust me down, apologising profusely for their bad behaviour. I felt that we were accepted; from that moment the ghastly truck ride was completely transformed and became thoroughly enjoyable.

We bumped our way on to the Cizre road at the village of Midyat. The coach was due to leave in half an hour, so that we just had time for a quick meal and a wash of sorts before leaping on board. I spent the journey back pondering gloomily the problem of how we were to get *Hermes* to Nusaybin. Hiring a truck was going to be expensive, always assuming that we still had a boat to be trucked.

We arrived back at Cizre at 7.30 that evening. As we walked back towards *Hermes* I noticed the villagers were giving us a curious look, a peculiar knowing smile, sly and hostile. At first glance she looked intact; the outboard, transmitter, batteries, food and fuel canisters were still there. It wasn't until later that night that we found we had lost a sleeping bag, an expensive quilted sailing jacket, three shirts, 200 feet of rope, water canisters, an alarm clock, and a variety of cooking utensils. We had one thought—and one thought only—out.

I found most of the truck owners sitting on some old wooden chairs outside a dirty little tea-stall. Carrying my glass of sweet milkless tea, I went over to join them. But when I mentioned my hiring a truck, they froze. Eventually one of them quoted some astronomical figure. They knew our position and wanted all or nothing.

Feeling thoroughly miserable and dejected I went back to the boat, to find Dave preparing a meal from a packet of Heinz dehydrated food. I was becoming weaker with dysentery; after only three days of it I could feel my strength ebbing and with it, my patience. The heat, our exhaustion and the tension caused by being in such a serious position, were beginning to affect our relationship. Here on land I was no longer the experienced skipper; we were on equal terms. Dave was all for thumping hell out of the kids who kept trying to pinch our equipment, but I felt this would only worsen the situation. A number of short, sharp arguments ensued.

'For Christ's sake don't put their backs up any more.'

'But they're pinching our bloody gear.'

'They'll do a damn sight more if you hit them.'

'It's the only thing they bloody well understand.'

Eventually we both clammed up, silently nursing our convictions.

I was slowly turning over my food, not feeling very hungry, when a fat, gruesome-looking Turk waddled over, trying hard to put on a benevolent smile, wringing his two podgy hands together. He had heard in the village that we wanted someone to take us to Nusaybin; he would be pleased to do it for only 200 Turkish pounds. This was a fifth of the price that the others were asking. We could leave tonight and go by special road he knew through the mountains, right under the noses of the Syrians. We were overjoyed, and he left clutching a Turkish 100-pound note as a deposit. We were already packed to leave, when I bumped into Hassan, and began to explain the situation to him. As soon as I had described our new friend Hassan burst into laughter.

'You want yourself killed ? That man the worst focking bandit in this village. He take you to his focking family village twenty focking miles and kill you both, take your focking boat, everything.' I thought perhaps Hassan was over-dramatising the situation, but he took me along to the police headquarters, and they confirmed his story.

It was a narrow escape. Now we were back in our previous predicament of no transport, minus £10 that we could ill afford. Hassan again came to the rescue—his brother was just returning from a rather dubious run in his truck from Iraq and was due to arrive within a couple of hours. For 600 Turkish pounds he would take us to the train at Nusaybin by yet another road through the mountains; *Hermes* would be loaded as soon as his brother appeared, and we could leave at first light. Except for the price, this all sounded to be exactly what we wanted, but although Hassan gave us every impression of being our friend, I still had my suspicions. There was no doubt that he was a smuggler and a rogue, and I was uncertain of how far we could trust him, which was why I had not contacted him before. However, such was our predicament that we had to accept the risk.

The headlights of a vehicle could be seen sweeping and dipping over the horizon from the direction of the Iraqi border, before disappearing behind a hillock. A few minutes later they emerged again and swept across a narrow wooden bridge.

'This is my brother now.' Hassan left me sitting at a dirty wooden table sipping heavily sweetened tea. Ten minutes passed before he returned, arguing with a tall brawny Arab. 'My brother.' He spat out the words with distaste. 'He come back with six tons tobacco and tea over those roads. My truck only supposed to carry three tons. He wreck it one day. Come, we get some men, load up your boat.' Hassan's brother, whom we called Fred, was grinning all over his face. I stood up to shake his hand, and almost stumbled forward — I hadn't realised how weak I was. Standing against this tough young Arab I knew that we would be at his mercy. But somehow I didn't care any more; I just wanted to get to the Tigris and be on the move once more.

Six men were gathered around the boat, the same six who had off-loaded us. This time they wanted their money before work started, and twice as much as before. Cursing my weakness, I paid them without argument. Ropes were lashed over *Hermes* and fenders stuffed around the keel. Hassan told us to jump on and we drove off into the village.

When Hassan and his brother jumped down from the cab and walked into their house, it occurred to us that this was where we would stop for the night. We began to arrange our sleeping places, but five minutes later they both came out again with Hassan carrying a revolver. Without a word of explanation, ignoring our questioning glances, they jumped into the cab, started the engine and drove off.

'God, this is it,' Dave said, lowering his voice. 'Somewhere along the mountain road, miles from anywhere, they'll stop and we'll all disappear.' I felt that he was only too right, that our only chance lay in our native cunning. We weighed up the odds; we carried no arms, but could put many pieces of equipment to effective use. Rummaging about in the lockers I found four distress rockets. We also had a Very pistol but the two cartridges for it were too small and too long. They not only rattled from side to side in the barrel, but protruded two inches out of the nozzle; sadly we rejected them, on the grounds that we would do more damage to ourselves than to our enemies. Dave lined the rockets up astern; I grabbed the boat hook, always a good weapon in hand-to-hand combat. We were ready. I shuddered at the thought of having to kill someone. Looking across at Dave I realised that he felt the same way.

We reasoned that somewhere along the track, in a desolate area, they would stop. It was essential that we act first, to hold the advantage of surprise. Hassan was driving, and held the gun; as soon as the truck began to slow down, I would position myself above the cab; as he emerged, I could give him a hefty swipe with the boat hook, followed by a rocket. Dave could leap over the side and fire another rocket at the brother. By then I should have the gun and the tables would be turned to our advantage. We both agreed that no field-marshal could think of a better plan, and settled down ready for zero hour.

For three hours we sat there, tense and nervous, waiting. There were numerous false alarms, when the truck slowed down to take a bend. I was sitting on *Hermes'* side deck, thinking miserably that I was too young to die, when suddenly to either side houses began to appear. The truck slowed down, and in the excitement of seeing some sign of human habitation again we forgot all about our morbid plan. Slowly we rolled to a stop directly outside a small army garrison. Hassan and his brother jumped down and explained that since it was now two o'clock in the morning, we would go no farther tonight. They were going off to a hotel for some sleep and asked if we would like to join them. With complete abandonment, we both laughed. Our relief was such that we rolled around laughing our heads off. Eventually I recovered sufficiently to tell them we would stay with the boat. They walked off thinking us quite mad.

It was only later that it struck us just how serious the situation had been. If they had stopped along the road, if only to see that everything was in order behind—we dared not think of the consequences.

At nine o'clock that morning, after a quick breakfast of cheese and syrupy tea, we left the main road for Hassan's own route through the mountains. This was not a stone or dirt road, but straight across a wide open desert. The dust was unbearable; no matter where we positioned ourselves, this fine choking powder billowed around us. In place of our stolen water canisters we had boiled out some plastic fuel bottles to carry water in. The taste was obnoxious—they were still strongly contaminated with petrol; the water was lukewarm, but our mouths and throats were burning and we knew that we had to drink the foul liquid or dehydrate. Indeed we were beginning to sink into an obscene state beyond the imagination of any decently brought-up human being. We had not washed for weeks. Our clothes were wet and stank of sweat and the pungent, sickly smell of dysentery. To descend to such depths (lower than either of us had ever sunk before) is far from pleasant, and I knew that we would have to fight this off if we were to survive.

Later that afternoon we were negotiating the potholes in Nusaybin's main street for the second time in three days. Driving down beside the railway track, we off-loaded *Hermes* directly onto the wagon-loading ramp before the stationmaster could utter a word of complaint. This was it. Our only way to the Tigris and the Persian Gulf lay down this narrow railway track which ran directly across the Syrian border. It was our last chance, or this small, dusty station would be the end of the line for our voyage. I went along to see the stationmaster to ask him about a truck.

'The only truck we can give you is in Syria,' he replied in a mixture of French and English. 'I will send a telegram for them to bring it here, but when it arrives I don't know. Maybe one day, maybe two, maybe three days.' I smiled politely and walked back to where Dave was sitting under the sun awning alongside *Hermes*. 'This may be a long wait,' I said. 'Let's find someone to look after the boat, while we go along to that hotel in the village and get cleaned up. A good shower would do us the world of good.'

A young lad who worked on the railway promised to sleep by *Hermes* for ten Turkish pounds, about one pound sterling. Dave and I, carrying a large bag of dirty washing, walked into the village towards the hotel. We returned early the following morning, with a clean bag of washing and freshly showered. The lad was still there close alongside; he rose from the air bed we had loaned him and greeted us in Turkish. Another youth was with him and greeted us in English.

'Good morning,' he said, 'my friend here says that you do not pay him enough.'

'We are paying him what he asked, which I think is too much anyway,' I replied rather slowly.

'He now wants twenty pounds or he says he cause trouble,' said the newcomer. 'He has many friends,' he added with a sly smile. This was too much. We grabbed the lad who had been looking after *Hermes* and flung him against the brick wall of a near-by building.

'You tell him,' I spat, 'that he gets what we agreed. Nothing else. And if he tries to steal anything, I'll cut his bloody throat.' The sight of the two of us flushed with anger had the necessary effect. The youth stared back with terror written across his face, gurgling and mumbling something incomprehensible. I gave him ten Turkish pounds and told him to clear off, whereupon he ran like a scalded cat.

Our truck arrived on the third day, towed behind a two-carriage diesel passenger-train full of Arabs. Slowly the rusted wheels of bureaucracy turned; the official forms needed to leave Turkey began to flood in, and the closer we came to the point of leaving Turkey the more anxious I became about entering Syria. *Hermes* was loaded onto the wagon. All we needed now was the Baghdad Express, which arrived on the fourth evening. We made sure that *Hermes*' wagon was coupled up behind before going on board ourselves. For three days and nights we had lived alongside the railway track; entering an air-conditioned carriage was like crossing the borders of Hell into Heaven.

Nothing happened. We sat and waited at the station for four hours. It was now approaching midnight and still the train, with steam hissing from its belly, stayed immobilised just a few hundred yards from the Syrian border. A few more minutes passed and, suddenly, the express began to move. Within five minutes we had stopped again at another station, this time in Syria. I felt sick with anxiety. A dozen Syrian guards, customs and police officials came on board. They passed our compartment three or four times, but never came in. My thoughts were screaming, 'Move, train—move.' We were both tense with excitement, willing the train to start again. Slowly the minutes ticked by. Suddenly, at one o'clock in the morning, the silence was shattered by a piercing whistle, the carriages crashed together and the towing chains rang loudly in successive clangs as the strain was taken up by the engine. We were moving again—into Syria.

Dawn was just breaking as the express slowed down and finally stopped at the next station, still in Syria but on the Iraqi border. Again an armada of police and customs officials came on board and this time into our compartment. 'This is it,' I thought. We had no visas, we were not even supposed to be there, and our passports had a useless, insignificant stamp with 'In Transit' blotted on one corner of a page. 'Let's hope their prisons are clean,' I mumbled to Dave as we were marched off the train towards a small police office, which was crowded with Arabs shouting and gesticulating. The official behind the desk seemed tired of life. Our passports were handed over and he slowly flicked through the pages, holding them upside down, and working from the back. Fumbling into one of the desk drawers he produced a large rubber stamp and with one hefty thump produced a full page of red, Arabic figures and completed the pattern by scrawling all over it with his pen. From another drawer he took two postage stamps, which he licked absent-mindedly. Our passports were then handed back in exchange for the equivalent of two pounds in Syrian lire. 'Is that all they want from us ?' Dave whispered in my ear. 'Looks like it.' My hand was shaking as I looked at my passport and back to the police officer. 'Let's get the hell out of here.' We backed out of the office and walked quickly to the train. Once safely in our compartment we both slumped down in our seats, overcome with relief. I was trembling all over, with perspiration streaming down my face, even though we were in an air-conditioned carriage. 'We've done it,' I said. 'We've done it.'

When the famous express eventually shunted into Mosul station, it had taken a full twenty-four hours to travel the 100 miles from Nusaybin at an average speed of 4.16 miles per hour. We dropped down from our carriage on to the stony track, clutching our few overnight belongings wrapped in a small blue cotton bag. A young Pakistani who had shared our carriage followed us down and began to search methodically below the carriages. A large half-rotten tomato lay a few yards from us; beaming with delight, he swooped upon it and stuffed it into his mouth. I looked at Dave, who raised his eyebrows.

The wagon containing *Hermes* was unhitched and shunted into a siding; when we asked the railway officials how we could get her onto the river, we found that the first part of the operation was to get customs clearance. This sounded simple until we entered the customs building and began the form filling. The most difficult exercise lay in explaining to our civil service friends just what our mode of travel was. Everyone travelled through Iraq by air, road or rail, and so no other form or means of transport existed. This particular group of bureaucrats persisted in their assumption that our craft must have wheels if it was to proceed through to the Persian Gulf. After three days of constant arguing, we managed to convince them that we really intended to sail through, and that we were only slightly mad. They beamed in delight, gave us all the necessary documents and allowed us to proceed on our way.

During the spring flood, the Tigris is often half a mile to a mile wide. But looking down from the Mosul bridge we could see that it was only 50 yards across, and littered with many shallow banks. It was now 12 August—one month later than planned—and I wondered uneasily if the river was going to be navigable. To our advantage, however, was the fact that we had missed the 100 miles of the upper reaches by starting here at Mosul and not at Cizre. There was a chance that we might be in luck.

To transport *Hermes* to the Tigris, we hired a truck and half a dozen Arab helpers and within half an hour were driving down towards the river bank. I was convinced that after all her violent and rough handling, *Hermes* would sink like a stone as soon as she touched the water. But my tough little craft needed more than a 500-mile truck journey to sink her. She slid into the cool swift-flowing waters and floated as buoyantly as ever, straining on her mooring warp, eager to be on the move once more in her natural environment.

On tow behind a barge on the Tigris

The skipper of the barge, who asked for tablets to make him fit to satisfy his three wives;
I gave him twelve vitamin tablets

When we stayed in an Arab village with Bedouin camp close by

Hermes at Bahrain after being smashed up on the river Tigris

8

THE AFTERNOON SHADE TEMPERATURE HAD ALREADY REACHED 115°F and was still rising. We raised the masts, stretched a sun awning between them, and busied ourselves with the loading of fuel and fresh provisions. More of our own dry foodstuffs were being flown out to Bahrain by the RAF, 1200 miles ahead; as a precaution against the rapids that were threatened in the first section of river, we loaded on board a mass of blocks and tackle and long terylene warps.

Sweating profusely, I sat down for a moment to look at the map; for the first 250 miles signs of human habitation were few and far between. Hundreds of miles of desert wasteland spread out to either side of the river banks; according to my researches in London nothing grew here during the summer months except for a few crops of coarse, spiney camel grass. I wondered for the umpteenth time if my decision to use the Tigris as our road to the Persian Gulf was the right one. Our chances of survival were dim, if anything should happen to us; if the boat was wrecked in a rapid, or either of us fell seriously sick, help would be too far away for us to survive for long. The customs officials in Mosul had warned us repeatedly of the scorpions and spiders and snakes, the only living creatures in these barren wastes; now their crude, cruel habitat was about to be invaded by two sick, weak and half-mad British subjects in their strange bright yellow craft.

Late that afternoon, as the oil city of Mosul receded into the distance, I began to reflect upon the next 1000 miles down this historic water course. There was an atmosphere of tension and excitement on board *Hermes* at the prospect of our being the first two Europeans to navigate this river; a real feeling of adventure, like two intrepid pioneers on a voyage of discovery.

The first few hours passed uneventfully; the river, although running fast, had enough smooth areas of water where navigation was relatively easy. From time to time it split into three, but I could see at a glance that only one of these arms would be deep enough for *Hermes*; the others would be either too shallow or too rocky, and many were merely branches leading off into the wilderness. The sun dipped below the shimmering desert, and we motored on into the dusk; meandering along, keeping close to the bank for fear of losing ourselves.

I was sitting at the helm, savouring the coolness of the night, while Dave was preparing some food. Somewhere in the dark void ahead, I heard a sound like wind rustling through the trees. Except that in these parts there are no trees. The rocky bank began to slip by faster, the soft sighing became louder, until I suddenly recognised the roar of water cascading down a rapid. Flickers of white began to shine through the blackness ahead, the foam and froth of a river gone mad into a turmoil of seething white water. Helming with the outboard at full revs made no difference to our course. We were in the grip of the rapid.

'Hang on! Hang on!' I shouted to Dave. The bows dipped, rose and twisted, as large, ugly, jagged rocks slipped by on both sides. Then—*crunch*, the sickening sound of splitting wood. Silence. Hurling food, cooking pots and clothing to one side, we both frantically tore up the bottom boards. The bilge was already half full of water and plenty more was coming in through a lengthy crack in the plywood on the bottom planking. I swung *Hermes* round and ran her straight for the bank.

Caulking cotton, a heavy screwdriver and a hammer were raked out from the stern locker. It wasn't that it was a difficult job; what disturbed me was that we had suffered our first serious damage within hours of setting off on this river. How many more rapids lay ahead? Was this river really unnavigable ? 'No wonder nobody has ever sailed down this bloody river before,' I said as I hammered in the caulking cotton.

We decided to stay moored alongside the bank for the rest of the night; our air beds were punctured, and we lay on the hard bottom boards under the mosquito net. My mind was in a turmoil. Any idea of travelling by night obviously had to be abandoned, and the dangers ahead were now only too real. The farther we progressed the farther we were going into a barren and hostile land. Besides this accursed dysentery, there were the mosquitoes to compete with. If we had to work in the river there were the bilharzia, small grub-like worms that eat away at the human bowel; there was also the heat, which had killed only too many in the past. On the other hand, if we could not cope with these difficulties during this comparatively short section of the voyage, there was little point in our continuing. But to turn back was unthinkable.

Later next morning we came across our second rapid. This time we were prepared; 100 yards upstream I put into the bank and walked down to take a good look. It was obviously an old barrage. Before Iraq became a republic, the lands were split up into sheikhdoms. To keep the surrounding lands fertile during the dry season, crude barrages of earth and rock were thrown across the river to hold back the water and irrigate the land. This was one of these barrages, now in a sad state of disrepair; it had been broached in three places and the river dropped six feet the other side into a white boiling foam. Of the three, the inside passage seemed the better bet for us; it was over ten feet wide, twice the width of the other two; and the drop wasn't quite so steep. But there were still plenty of sharp plank-splitting boulders strewn about. We took bearings on the various obstacles, to establish the best direction to steer. Once in the mighty grip of this torrent *Hermes* would obviously run in the direction the river wanted to take her, but we stood a better chance if we could line her up accurately for the deepest section before coming into its influence.

I waded back to the boat, trying not to think of the bilharzia, and clambered on board. We gently eased her out into the main stream and slowly lined ourselves up on a couple of withies I had placed at strategic points. The river was only three feet deep and I could already see large grey rocks slipping by below our keel at an increasing rate of knots. Each one seemed to be reaching up in an attempt to smash the boat into minute fragments. *Hermes* ceased to answer to my helming. We were in the grip, past the point of no return. No point in staying on the helm, so I leaped over the side and hung onto the gunwale, my legs ready to fend off any rocks that came too close. We shot through the gap like a bullet, and she went wild in the stopper waves below. It was all I could do to hang on, kicking frantically at the rocks as they swept past. Twice I heard a thud as we hit submerged boulders and envisaged myself thumping some more caulking cotton into the split planks. The river dragged us along, over and past the rocks into deep water once more. We both climbed back on board and I headed *Hermes* in towards the bank. We spent the next half hour inspecting the damage and to my great relief I found that we had got away with only a few bruised planks and the odd grazed shin. 'We've been bloody lucky, Dave,' I said as I climbed back on board. 'There's no doubt about it, she's a tough little boat.'

'I'll second that,' he replied as he pushed *Hermes*' bow away from the bank.

We were both beginning to think that we could now tackle anything that this river had to offer. Rapids, barrages and fast-flowing gulleys had all been negotiated without too many problems, all of them offering various degrees of excitement and taxing our powers of initiative. We were beginning to feel a little cocky when suddenly, while motoring down a 400-yard-wide section of the river, we ground to a halt. A sickening and very definite halt. Ahead lay a 200-yard stretch of shingle with a bare six inches of water covering it. 'Only one way across this, mate,' I said, as cheerfully as I could. 'Dig a channel. But all we've got to dig the channel with are those two wooden oars.'

This was a problem that required sheer manpower, but the best that I could offer was half a man. The cursed dysentery had weakened me so much that it was as much as I could do to hold an oar, let alone dig with it. Dave had also been suffering from the odd bout, but it had never taken hold of him as it had with me.

Without a word Dave unlashed the oars from their stowage place between the forestay and the shrouds. The temperature was up to 120°F, as we began to dig away slowly at the hard, compact, stony river bed. A normal healthy man could have made more of an impression with a pocket knife. As I dug, almost blinded by sweat, I noticed the river swirling around *Hermes*. The force of the water around her caused an eddy that scoured out a small hollow directly below her bows. For once I blessed the river, which was helping us at last. All we had to do was make that hollow wider.

It was asking too much. Ten minutes' work in that heat was enough. We collapsed and wallowed in the cool waters of the river, in a state of total exhaustion. But as I looked around at our parched, inhospitable surroundings, I realised that somehow, from somewhere, we would have to find the strength to continue; otherwise we should die. Without any shadow of a doubt, we should die.

We got back to work. Slowly we scraped away a little more at the shingle bank. With the sweat streaming down my face and body I looked up for a moment. The sun blazed down on the parched sand and rock banks which stretched away to the foot of barren sandstone cliffs. Our nearest help was at Mosul, over 100 miles to the north; Tikrit, the next village, was 150 miles to the south. The nearest town eastwards was over 200 miles and to westwards, over 500 miles. Our only chance of reaching civilisation, if we had to abandon *Hermes*, was in the life raft; this we could easily manhandle over the shallows, and we could drift with the current down to Tikrit. If we tried walking we might survive 10 miles. *Hermes* would have to be left to rot.

The mere thought of it was enough to get us working again. No matter what happened, we could never leave her now. For four hours we dug and scraped, heaved and pushed; the sweat streamed down our bodies until I thought there could be no more moisture left in us. We drank gallons of river water laced with salt, past caring what disease-carrying bugs lived in it. Back to the digging, feebly heaving the boat forward a few inches at a time. Neither of us knew when we reached the end; suddenly, as we were hauling her through the channel we had dug, we noticed that she was free. We were too tired to speak. We clambered back on board; while Dave stowed the oars, I reached back to start the outboard motor.

It no longer lay within us to reason why we were going to Australia. To get there had become a job of work, no more and no less. Our present difficulties on the Tigris were just obstacles in the performance of completing a duty—we were beyond the stage of being interested or getting excited. They were jobs that had to be tackled. The next few days passed in a dream, as we forced our way down the river, negotiating each rapid or shallow as it came along as a daily routine—a routine that was no different from eating and sleeping, which we struggled to perform silently and monotonously. By the morning of 15 August the dysentery had sapped every ounce of strength from my body. The pills I had been given by my doctor in England were having no effect. At first I could not rise; when I eventually managed to sit up, my head swirled and my stomach cried out for mercy from the racking, gnawing pains. The muscles seemed to twist and contort so agonisingly that I wished I could tear my stomach out. I pulled out the map. Tikrit was only 15 miles downstream; in Tikrit we hoped that we might find help. According to a contact back in London a Scottish couple lived there, a Mr and Mrs Donald, the husband being the resident engineer for a contracting company building a bridge across the river. 'I hope to God they haven't left by now,' I said weakly, lying back in the bottom of the boat. 'We're already over two months late. They could have finished the job. Or gone home on leave.'

After a few hours of motoring we began to notice the odd mud hut, mostly deserted, their walls crumbling into decay. A few miles farther and the houses became inhabited and were built of sand or limestone bricks with mud as mortar, the first we had seen for seven days and 250 miles. Our hopes began to rise further. Then, around a sharp bend, we saw signs of a bridge under construction.

I eased the boat alongside a steep bank where a crowd of young Arab students were bathing. As I stumbled ashore, I asked them, panting for breath, the way to the offices of the construction site. One of the young lads caught me by the arm and held me steady. I thanked him, but pushed his arm to one side. In perfect English he offered to show me the way and walked off, while I stumbled behind, my head whirling and my stomach crying out with the pain. Soon we came to a group of white office buildings, and I noticed a thermometer hanging in the shade of a veranda. It read 126°F. A young Polish engineer directed me to one of the offices; as he opened the door I almost collapsed and had to be helped to a chair. Inside it was blissfully cool, thanks to the air-conditioning. I slowly came to my senses to see Mr and Mrs Donald standing over me with a selection of ice-cold drinks. The doctor was called and I was sent straight to bed with a mass of tablets to be taken four times a day, plus an old Scottish remedy prescribed by Mrs Donald, half a tumbler of good Scotch whisky.

In the meantime, Dave found himself in a sticky position with the Arab students. To show as much courtesy as possible we had lashed the whip aerial on to the mizzen mast with the Iraqi flag tied to the very top. Convinced that we were sending out radio reports, the young Arabs were busy accusing Dave of being a spy, issuing dire warnings that we would both be strung up as soon as we reached Baghdad. It was a silly thing to do on our part, but we were unaccustomed to the childish suspicions that exist in these parts of the world. Later that afternoon, while I was lying in bed, there was a knock at the front door. I heard Mrs Donald answer it and a lengthy conversation ensued, after which she came up to my room and explained that one of the students must have informed on us. The local secret police had been asking questions. Fortunately the authorities must have been satisfied with Mrs Donald's answers, because the whole affair died down as quickly as it had arisen.

Through the kindness of our new friends, I began to build up my strength again over the next few days, and the worst of the dysentery began to disappear. Dave recovered from his minor attack in the first day. Even though I was not completely better, I was at least strong enough to continue the voyage. It was a case of necessity as we still had 750 miles to go down river and only sixteen days left on our visas. When the time came to leave, there was no way in which I could thank the Donalds enough. Without a doubt they had saved my life with their nursing, and with no reward to themselves.

After Tikrit the going was good. The river was now deep and wide with few difficulties and our spirits were only dampened by the almost intolerable heat. Villages, usually a cluster of mud houses, became a frequent sight; each group of huts was set on a small hillock, formed from the remains of other settlements, where, after a few years, through winter rains and the summer's blistering heat and sandstorms, they would slowly erode away to their original state of mud and sand. The villagers would then spend a week erecting new homes, and the cycle would continue. After 200 years, some of the hillocks would be as much as 100 feet high.

These Arabs, unlike those we met in the towns, still kept, in their crude but pleasant communities, the charm and kindness of the original Arab—before they had been corrupted by western influence. We now began to experience the true hospitality of the Arab people; as we passed, the villagers hailed us from the bank inviting us ashore. At first, since we had little time to spare, we placed our right hands across our hearts and muttered, 'Sorry—but we haven't enough time,' or something to that effect, hoping that this would convey our appreciation for their thoughtfulness and our regrets. One morning a particularly cheerful group hailed us and we decided to stop. Helping hands took our painter and steadied us ashore. The head man of the village was the local schoolmaster, a youthful and handsome thirty-year-old who spoke good English and invited us to his home. Noticing my concern for *Hermes*, he assured me that all would be well; with some reluctance I accepted this and we followed him through the dusty village street.

In contrast to the towns we had already visited, the small cluster of mud and stone houses was surprisingly clean. The narrow streets, although made of just sand and stone, were not littered with rubbish, nor was there the usual stream of black putrefying liquid running down the centre, nor the sweet sickly smell. Each house had a small backyard with a number of chickens running about freely, pecking at pieces of unleavened bread discarded after the morning meal. Wood for the cooking fires was stacked tidily in one corner, the earth grates were swept clean and the cooking pots stacked neatly alongside. None of these houses had a lavatory or washing facilities, but the river was only a few yards away.

In strict Muslim tradition, the women scuttled outside as soon as we entered his house, accompanied by much giggling. By now quite a crowd had gathered and most of them followed us into the long room with rough whitewashed walls. The floor was of hard-packed earth, and a long narrow carpet ran around the edge of the room. Numerous hard cushions were placed at six-foot intervals on this carpet, while at the far end stood a large, perspiring earthenware water jar, a continuous stream of dew-like droplets dripping with monotonous regularity into a bowl beneath. A bowl of food was brought in, fried eggs swimming in oil, and with the help of unleavened bread we began to dig in with our hands. Sour milk diluted with the cool water from the earthenware jar proved a most refreshing drink, very much like liquefied yoghurt.

To us the scene was strange and wonderfully fascinating. It was the first time we had been received in an Arab home and I was concerned that we should act in the correct manner. I had already made one mistake when we first entered; the head man had asked us to be seated and through complete ignorance I sat on the pile of cushions that we were only supposed to lean against. Seeing how the Arabs were seated, I slowly eased myself down onto the carpet.

While we were eating, questions were being fired at us from the crowd, both inside and outside the room. Eventually we heard the one that we had been dreading. 'What do the British people regard as the solution to the Palestinian/Arabs fighting against the Jews?' translated our host.

'I'm sorry, but that's something that I have never really studied,' I replied, speaking rather quietly. Mercifully they accepted this and the conversation wandered off on to the difficulties of farming in such a hot and dry climate.

In the heat of the afternoon we settled down for a siesta inside the cool of the hut. Our beds were the carpets around the walls, our pillows the hard cushions covered in beautiful hand-woven tapestry. At six o'clock the village came to life once more and our host took us along to the small village bazaar, in a long, low, white building with coloured striped awnings leading out halfway across the dusty main street. The goods were spread out underneath the awnings and the market was divided up into three sections, one for cooking pots and household utensils, the second for cloth and carpets and the third for food: water melons, eggs and caged live chickens. It being midsummer, the middle of the dry season, vegetables and fruit were scarce.

As darkness approached, we made our farewells. Our host insisted on accompanying us as we strolled down to *Hermes*. Maybe I was half-expecting to find her stripped of everything. But I certainly felt deeply ashamed, when I thanked the old man with an ancient Lee-Enfield, who had been dutifully guarding the boat ever since we arrived. I was learning the hard way.

Early the following morning we spotted Samarra ahead. We could see the golden dome of a mosque and the spiral tower of one of the largest minarets in the Middle East towering over the low river bank. Here lay one of our last major obstacles, a large concrete barrage built back in the 1930s by the British for irrigating the vast expanses of desert on either side. We had heard back in Tikrit that a German construction company was building a hydro-electric power station alongside, and I hoped that they would have a large crane that we could borrow for a short while to hoist *Hermes* over the obstruction.

As we approached Samarra, numerous Arabs working along the river bank began to call out to us, warning us about the barrage ahead. But we had no intention of being sucked into it and spewed out the other side in tiny fragments. Just before the barrage I noticed a small police-boat pen alongside the river bank; obviously this was the place to leave *Hermes* while we went off in search of the German contractors. The bridge over the barrage was guarded at both ends by police. When I walked up to a uniformed police official and showed him our papers and passports, he seemed satisfied and allowed us to cross.

The barrage was about the length of Putney Bridge and the river was as wide as the Thames at that point. It was deep, wide and swift-flowing; the banks on the far side began to show signs of greenery, and the odd bush or tree gallantly tried to add a splash of colour to the parched land. Outside the prefabricated office block at the far end was a ten-ton mobile crane. Just what we wanted, in fact. All we needed to do now was to convince our German friends that our cause was a deserving one.

We had nothing to fear. In a matter of minutes the crane, a three-ton truck, a bulldozer and twelve men were all placed at our disposal. In command of the operation was a young Australian electrician called John, who was about the same age as myself, and who was just bubbling over at the chance to speak English once more. 'But first of all you had better go back and bring her across. One of my lads will give you a hand.'

A young Arab lad ran up behind to follow me across. As I was walking down the steps, my spirits sank. I could see at a glance that something was very wrong. Our equipment was scattered about all over the cockpit, locker doors were open, clothing pulled out. But worse was in store. Underneath the mess was a briefcase which had been stowed well into the forward locker, and which was now empty. All the papers had gone, and with them £50 in sterling, our standby currency. I let out a long stream of oaths. 'You bloody, thieving, bleeding, Arab pigs,' I screamed. From the top of the steps I noticed three policemen looking down. When they saw that I was looking at them, they turned away quickly. It was obvious that they were the culprits—the only possible culprits. But what could I do? The loss was critical, but I realised that we would never get our money back however long we stayed. It was another hard and bitter lesson learned.

John's young Arab cast off the mooring warps, and we motored out into the river. When we were halfway across, the outboard began to cough and splutter. He looked at me nervously, but I was too mad about the money to worry about the outboard. It often used to cough and splutter, thanks to the low-grade, sludge-like oil we had to use, but the motor had yet to give up completely because of this. We began to drift ominously towards the sluice gates. The lad stared wide-eyed at the barrage, transfixed by the water swirling around its gates. His mouth opened and closed emitting a low garbled sound that I took to be a Muslim prayer. After a couple of minutes the engine got over its coughing spasm and we completed the crossing.

A bulldozer was hitched onto a warp tied to *Hermes*, and she was pulled clear of the water up the deep sandy river bank to the roadway. The crane then took over, hoisting her up onto a three-ton truck, which ran around the side of the barrage. The crane then lifted her off into the river the other side. The whole process was quick, simple and easily accomplished with typical German efficiency. When she was bobbing around in the swirling swift waters on the south side of the barrage, John called out to us to come ashore for a drink. Unfortunately *Hermes* was lying close to a bank of large sharp boulders and I was afraid that if we left her she would damage herself severely. I explained our predicament, and we agreed to meet again in Australia.

A hundred miles south of us lay Baghdad, two days' journey with the river now running wide and deep. We began to see more signs of life; numerous ferries ran across from one bank to the other, ranging from large motorised catamarans capable of carrying trucks and cars, to dug-out canoes with or without a ragged sail, and even one man drifting down river on an inflated goat skin. Heavily populated villages appeared around every bend, and we could hear well in advance the steady thump-thump of a single-cylinder diesel used for irrigation. Every farmer had one or two such engines, which were their pride and joy, and British into the bargain.

As we passed one of these villages, the children bathing in the river shouted and waved to us as we went by, and their elders on the bank joined in the shouting and laughing. We waved back, happy to ignore the fact that we were a strange sight to these people. I had done a two-hour session on the helm, and felt I had been exposed to the sun for long enough—the awning only gave shelter to the one off watch. I settled down on the bottom boards to try to get some sleep. Within minutes Dave was giving me a nudge with his foot. 'Someone wants us on shore, I guess. Shall we go in?' Before I had time to sit up, I heard the ominous crack of a rifle shot and some irate yelling from the shore. My decision to surrender took less than a second to make; I took the helm and headed into the bank.

A dirty, cross-looking Arab, brandishing an old Lee-Enfield 303, stood waiting for us, fuming with rage. As we approached he began to jump up and down, screaming at us in a totally incomprehensible language. Most of the villagers had gathered around, looking on with solemn faces. I gathered all our papers, visas and passports together, and was about to offer them up for his inspection, when he grabbed me by the arm and strode with me through the village to an old battered Ford. I looked back at Dave, who shrugged his shoulders. We wondered whether we would ever see one another again.

I was thrown into the back seat and my escort leapt in beside me. A few curt orders to the driver, a crash of gears, and we were speeding up the rocky road towards another village on the horizon. Eventually we pulled up outside a small white garrison, where I was manhandled out of the car and marched towards an office. At least this was a police post, not a bandit hideout. A police officer in uniform sat behind a desk, and with a smile held out his hand, dismissing my Gestapo escort with the other.

'Why didn't you stop at this village when you were told to?' he asked

Hermes repaired at Bahrain

Indian trader near Bombay

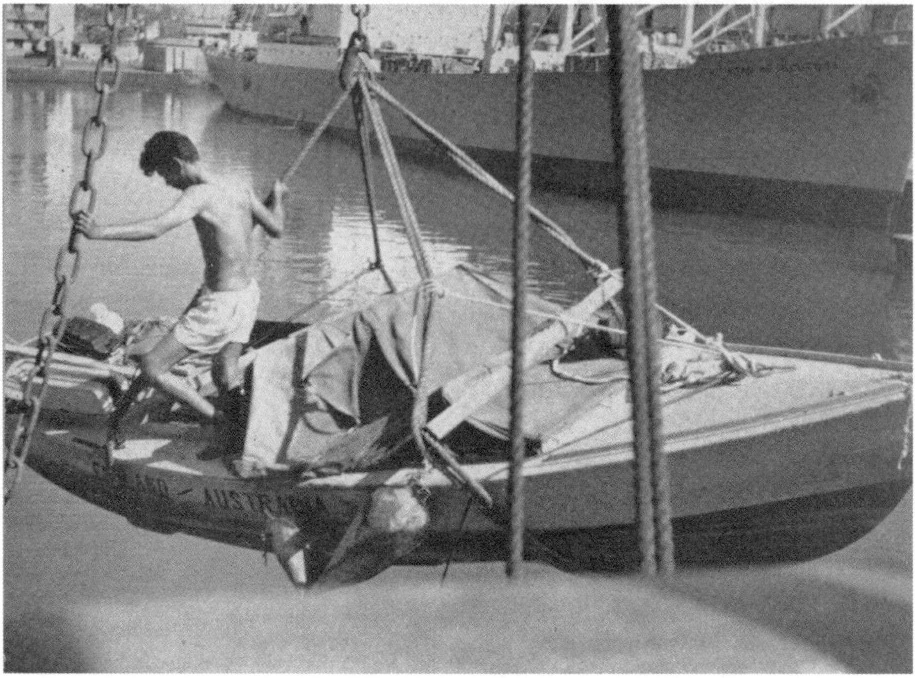

Load up onto MV *Chinkoa* for Penang, with an Indian helper

Nell

in perfect English. At once it dawned on me that somewhere amongst the crowd of children waving to us from the bank there had been a police officer calling us in; but since he wasn't wearing uniform, we had had little chance of recognising him.

'I'm sorry, but we saw so many people waving at us that we didn't realise one was a police officer.' He laughed, apologised for the inconvenience this had caused us, and offered me a glass of tea. The Gestapo escort was called in; after a few words with the officer, he, too, became more friendly. Almost as though making amends, he went out and bought me a large water melon, and then hailed the driver to take me back to *Hermes*.

All this time, Dave had been thinking that he might have to continue the voyage on his own, but when I returned I found that he had been treated to the usual village hospitality. Tea and food was being handed around, and everyone was happy. As we left, the villagers apologised once again for any rudeness and ill-treatment that we had received from the police; once more my heart opened to these people.

Ten miles downstream we reached an easy stretch of river, with earth banks rising steeply for ten feet on either side. I was on the helm, keeping close into the bank as I negotiated a bend, when I looked up into the muzzle of another rifle. With a bandolier of cartridges round his shoulders and a large curved dagger in his waist, a fearsome-looking Arab was jumping up and down, presumably in some sort of dance. He disappeared, to be replaced by another, similarly dressed. Steering out into the main stream, I stood up. Over two dozen of them were dancing and chanting away to the accompaniment of drums. I was tempted to stop, but thought better of it. No sooner had we sighted them than we rounded the bend and they were lost to sight.

'What the hell was that?' said Dave, standing alongside.

'Must be some celebration. Want to go back and find out?'

'Next time, perhaps.'

Half a mile farther on, a lone figure of an Arab waved to us from the far bank. He obviously wanted a lift across the river, so I brought *Hermes* round and motored across. We greeted each other by placing our right hand across our hearts. When he began to chatter away in Arabic, I pointed to the fore deck and he realised we could not understand. When he climbed on board, I reversed away from the bank and motored across to the other side, whereupon he jumped onto the bank. Turning around with a smile, he then pointed to us, drew his right index finger across his throat and pointed once more up stream.

'He wants to cut our bloody throats,' said Dave.

'Looks like it. Time to go, I think.' I waved to our guest, pointed downstream and then to my watch. Alas, we had no time. I threw the outboard into reverse, swung into mid-stream, and motored off as fast as possible. We found out later that this sign really means that a sheep or goat had been slaughtered and that a feast was in progress. Our friend was inviting us to the celebrations. Oh well, next time.

As we approached Baghdad we began to see the odd palm grove with clusters of dates hanging from the branches. Already they were a golden brown, rapidly ripening in the sun. Some farmers were already picking them, perched precariously at the tree tops selecting the riper strings. Hidden in some of the palm groves we frequently glimpsed an old sheikh's palace, with high white walls surrounding an inner courtyard. But what had once been splendid gardens were overgrown; now, sadly, the only inhabitants of these magnificent buildings are the local goats and asses.

Baghdad: tall blocks of concrete buildings on the horizon, iron bridges spanning the river, with a solid British last-for-ever look stamped on each one. Our friends in Tikrit had suggested we stop at the British Embassy, conveniently situated on the river bank, so that all we had to do was to look for the Union Jack. It wasn't hard to find. As we pulled into the jetty an elderly Arab took our mooring warps and guided us into the building.

We were greeted with a blast of cool air, and a smell of furniture polish and disinfectant that made our nostrils twitch. But ours were not the only ones to twitch. Above the smell of the polish there was the unmistakable whiff of sewer coming from somewhere. To his credit, the official on duty didn't bat an eyelid, but eventually gave the game away with a slight flicker of his nostrils. After a short wait, during which tea was served, we were shown into a large impressive room, carpeted from wall to wall, with big heavy mahogany furniture. It was done in good taste, to uphold the image.

The Chargé d'Affaires came across with a friendly greeting; when we had settled ourselves into deep luxurious arm chairs, he mentioned how he had heard about us from the Foreign Office in London, and that we hoped to meet the President, Al-Bakr. 'Frankly, I don't see much hope of this coming off, but I'll certainly inform the Iraqi officials that you're here. In the meantime, you're welcome to stay at the British Club.'

We spent the next few days on a full-scale recuperation campaign; we were both surprised to find how thin and tired we were—in two weeks I had lost two and a half stone in weight. Before leaving England I had been a fairly strong swimmer, but all I could manage now was one length of the small swimming pool in the British Club's grounds. The club itself, set in spacious grounds, was a mansion positively reeking with old colonial atmosphere. The large entrance hall, with the fans slowly whirling overhead, was furnished with deep leather-upholstered chairs; the small polished wood tables always had their dated copies of *Punch*, *Illustrated London News*, and *Country Life* neatly stacked on top. Servants, dressed from head to toe in white, scuffled around with drinks or trays of tea to small groups of members, either in the entrance hall, or under a sun awning around the swimming pool.

Our host was James Hopgood, the local Cook's representative, who really put himself out looking after us. He took us to his friends' houses for meals, to the British Embassy for film shows, and to a club/restaurant frequented only by Europeans for drinks. One day we sped in his ancient Cadillac down to Babylon, to see the Hanging Gardens, one of the Seven Wonders of the World. During this trip we must have been a considerable worry to him. Anyone who travels in and out of Baghdad by road has to pass military check points, where passports and visas are scrutinised and the car is often searched. With us we had a mass of cameras, including a forbidden 16-mm cine camera which Dave continuously had poking out of the car window, filming anything that moved. As we left Baghdad and approached the military check point, the cameras were hidden behind the front seats; we were not stopped, and drove straight through. But on our return journey an army guard came out into the road and waved us to a halt. James looked glum—if they found the cameras, more than the film would be confiscated. We handed our passports through the window, and the guard fumbled through them, first upside down, then back to front.

'You are from England,' he asked, almost spitting out the last word.

'No,' said James politely, 'we are from Britain—Great Britain.' The guard looked at him sternly, and slowly a smile crept across his face. He handed back the passports and we drove back into the city.

Four restful days slipped by before we had a note from the British Embassy, informing us that President Al-Bakr would see us at 10.30 the following morning. Panic stations: what could we wear? We managed to fish out from our bags a pair of white ducks each—not exactly made to measure, but good enough—and two fairly clean shirts. We even found a couple of ties. We hoped he wouldn't look at our feet. My leather shoes were covered in a green mould, a particularly tenacious mould which survived a whole tin of brown polish.

At 10.00 on the morning of 23 August we rattled towards the palace in a dilapidated, rust-infested Ford Consul taxi. While the palace was still only a speck on the horizon we came to our first check point, a barrier of barbed-wire, a small tank and half a dozen heavily armoured men. We had to negotiate two more before we arrived at the palace gates. Tanks, Jeeps, military trucks of all descriptions were parked along the wide road, and even in the palace gardens, camouflaged close to flower beds. Machine-gun posts, in sandbagged emplacements, were positioned at strategic points, making the palace an impenetrable fortress. Groups of heavily armed men, wearing camouflaged battle-dress, wandered around the weeping willows and chrysanthemums. President Al-Bakr was obviously a very worried man.

We dismissed the taxi at the palace steps and climbed up to the main entrance. Under my arm I carried a parcel wrapped in a shimmering light green foil: a long flower-patterned silk dressing gown, a gift for the President from the London Silk Centre. Every time we had stopped at a military check point I had expected them to take this away and look inside; but they had ignored it. Still nobody questioned it, even as we were shown into a large gilded room within the palace to await the convenience of the President. Tea was served, followed by small cups of the bitter, heavily scented coffee. We sat and waited, periodically nodding pleasantly at the heavily armed guards, and even receiving the occasional smile in return.

For over two hours we sat in that room, gradually reducing the Iraqi Republic's stockpile of American cigarettes. My hands, holding the parcel, became damp and the dye from the cheap wrapping paper that we had bought in Baghdad began to come off, leaving a blue smear across my palms. Eventually a distinguished-looking Arab dressed in a Savile Row suit came in, whispered to the army officer seated at a desk by the door, and walked across to us.—'I am General Al-Bakr's private secretary. Please come this way.' As we followed him down a long impressive hallway, I looked down at what had once been an expensive hand-woven Persian carpet, now almost threadbare through the continuous tramping of army boots. Soldiers in camouflage uniform, with sten guns held carelessly in their hands, were positioned every eight feet either side of the corridor. Still no one questioned my parcel.

'The President can only see you for ten minutes,' the secretary said as we stood outside the door. 'I will act as interpreter for whatever questions you may wish to ask.' But what questions had we to ask? We couldn't just sit there dumbly twiddling our thumbs. Before I had a chance to think any up, the door was opened and there before us was General Ahmed Hassan Al-Bakr, President of the Republic of Iraq.

He was sitting behind a large mahogany desk, bent over a number of papers, busily writing. As we approached he glanced up and peered through his eyebrows at us for a few seconds before returning to this writing. He looked about ten years older than in the official photographs, somewhere in his mid~50s; a well-built figure, dressed in a smart western light grey suit, with a serious, businesslike face topped with greying hair. We went forward and greeted him with some inconsequential pleasantries. He said nothing, and glowered at us again as though he carried the burden of the whole world on his shoulders. To our relief the secretary asked us to be seated on a victorian-style settee. The President then spoke in Arabic for a while to our interpreter, which gave me the chance to look around the room. My eye was caught by a round mahogany table with a glass top supported by beautifully bound copies of Dickens and Robert Louis Stevenson. The interpreter was now speaking in English. 'His Excellency would like to know the purpose of your voyage through Iraq.' As I spoke my piece about our following the silk trading route, I watched the President's face. He began to look a bit bored.

'I spent a few years in England in youth work,' I said, hoping that a change of subject would lighten the atmosphere. 'Perhaps His Excellency could tell us what Iraq is doing for the youth of her country?' When the interpreter had translated the question, the President began to address us. Neither Dave nor I could understand much Arabic, so we just smiled and nodded at suitable points through his speech. After a quarter of an hour, when the President had finished, our interpreter took approximately 30 seconds to tell us of a youth camp which had been set up twenty miles south of Baghdad.

We had already been with the President for double our allotted time, but I could see that he was obviously interested in this subject. So far he had not shown the slightest flicker of a smile and I was determined to leave on a friendly note.

'What does his Excellency think of the long-haired youths and mini-skirted women of the western world?' I asked.

I seemed to have struck the jackpot. The President began to smile and spoke for another few minutes.

'His Excellency says that we in Iraq have found an answer to this problem. If we find their hair is too long, we shave their heads; and if the women's skirts are too short, we paint their legs black.'

It was time to leave. We rose from the sofa and I went across and handed our present to the President, who was still smiling, highly amused with his answer to our last question. We wished him good fortune and walked to the door.

Outside in the corridor we heard the frantic rustling of paper coming from the office. I could hardly help smiling at the thought of how, with all the tanks and soldiers lined up to prevent an attack by some large military organisation, two people like us had just walked straight in, carrying under one arm what could easily have been a bomb. But such a thought was ungracious, because back in the secretary's office we were both handed a silver Arabian dagger as a gift. This was a very pleasant surprise, and I shall always cherish it.

One of the presidential cars was put at our disposal and we were driven back to the British Club. We walked into the bar with a slight swagger, casually mentioning that we had just been having a chat with General Ahmed Hassan Al-Bakr. We brought out our daggers and laid them on the bar. In true British style the members present just smiled at us pleasantly and carried on with their drinking.

Since we had seen the President there was nothing to stop us from leaving. The following day James Hopgood drove us and our small bundle of valuables down to our boat, and we set off towards Al Kut, 100 miles south of Baghdad, the scene of bitter fighting between the British and the Turks in the 1914–1918 war. For many long months our troops lay under siege, with no escape and little chance of rescue, all because the river was unnavigable during the summer.

Palm groves became a more common sight now, and the thumping of the irrigation engines sounded day and night. For the first time since Mosul we began to experience strong winds blowing off the desert, bringing with them clouds of fine choking dust, so fine that it penetrated our lockers, even the plastic boxes containing the camera equipment. We donned our Arab-style headgear once more.

Our outboard was still acting up; fifty miles above Kut it stopped altogether. We drifted into the bank and began to strip down the fuel pump and carburettor, cleaning out the thick glue-like oil that had finally got the better of us. A small dug-out canoe with half a dozen children on board came alongside to watch the two mechanical genii at work. One of the children was trailing a large fish over the side. Beaming all over his face, he presented it to us. I was at a loss as to what to do. It must have weighed all of six pounds, a meal for quite a sizeable family; the boy looked so thin, yet he wanted us to have it as a present. I felt acutely embarrassed—we really couldn't take it. Another young Arab, standing on the bank, called across to us in schoolboy English. 'My friends they want you have fish. Why you not want it?'

I tried to explain that unless we went ashore and built a fire we had no way of cooking such a fish, and even then it was too much for both of us to eat. There was nothing for it: we had to refuse, even though we knew it would offend him. 'I thank you very, very much,' I said, 'but we would like you to have the fish. Thank you for offering it to us.' I felt very sad over the whole affair. We threw the outboard together as fast as possible and got under way again.

The following morning we motored up alongside a small wooden jetty, jutting out through some reeds half a mile upstream of the Kut barrage. A body of a cat drifted by, writhing and twisting as though in the last throes of death, but it had been dead for over a week and now, gnawing inside its body, were a large number of small black fish, which gave it the appearance of being still alive. These fish had been put into both the Tigris and Euphrates rivers to eat the water snails which play a major part in the breeding cycle of the Bilharzia worm.

Below Kut lay the great expanse of marshes inhabited by the Marsh Arabs; with the limited time we had available, we were keen to get into this area as soon as possible. The barrage at Kut was no problem as a large lock had been built to one side. In the lock at the same time as us was one of the small barges that ply their cargo from Baghdad to Basra. When the barge skipper made signs of offering us a tow as far as Amarra, I readily accepted. This would speed up our journey into the marsh and lake area in southern Iraq, 100 miles south of Kut, and save us money on fuel into the bargain.

Neither the skipper nor any of his crew of four could speak English, but we tried our best to communicate none the less. As a small gesture of thanks for their hospitality, I attempted to treat the skipper's leg. At some time he had cut this badly; it was swollen and looked a nasty mess. Our medical kit was my pride and joy; with the book of instructions we reckoned that we could have performed anything from a tooth extraction to an appendectomy. But opening the medical box to get some penicillin powder for the infected cut was a fatal mistake; within minutes the rest of the crew were lining up for treatment. One complained of a bad rash covering his body, so I gave him some cauterising cream; another had toothache, so he had a codeine tablet; the third felt listless and explained at some length that he could no longer satisfy his three wives, so I gave him a dose of vitamin tablets.

The following day the skipper came to me and showed me his leg: the swelling had gone and the cut was clean. I think I was even more surprised than he was, but I tried to keep a poker face, on the grounds that naturally I had expected this to happen. The man with the rash showed me that this had gone, but he asked for some more cream to apply himself. When I squeezed some out onto a piece of cotton wool, he hurried off into the engine room with it. Every three hours he came back and this performance was repeated. It wasn't until much later I gathered from the skipper that the poor chap had syphilis and was trying to treat himself; for that, alas, I could offer no cure.

Later that day we stopped at a village to wait for a pontoon bridge to open. My new reputation quickly went the rounds. Within minutes thirty or more Arabs of all ages were lined up by our barge, while the small cabin became a miniature surgery. I was in a dilemma; being totally unqualified, medically speaking, I did not want to give them any of our dangerous drugs. The solution was simple. As each complaint was explained to me in a very descriptive form of sign language, I paused for a moment in deep thought, before announcing my prescription. Everyone received the same in the end: four aspirins.

We arrived at Amarra that evening; early the next morning, having thanked our bargee friends, we left under our own steam once more. We quickly found that, as the river runs through the marshes, it becomes very narrow, winding its way around tortuous bends, skirting numerous lakes to the right and dense reed lands to the left. Navigation became even more difficult as the river divided into a number of tributaries, all the same depth and width. It was only the scars on the earth banks, where barges had hit, that gave us any indication that we were on the right branch of the river. The high earth banks slowly gave way to reeds, six to eight feet in height, which formed an impenetrable barrier to either side. The fear of becoming lost in this maze became more real to us now; we were often at a loss as to which tributary to take, and there were no scars to guide us. On many occasions the river widened into small lakes surrounded by a seemingly impenetrable reed wall; but by carefully watching the flow of the river, and following it, we always managed to find a way out.

In one of these small lakes we noticed that vast acres of reeds had recently been cut just above water level. Farther on we spotted the Arabs working in the reeds from their own peculiar craft. These are similar to the Newfoundland Banks dory, but made of skin or canvas that has been stretched over a light reed framework, and heavily tarred. We knew that a village was not far off, and after travelling for another mile we came into a large opening, with more than 500 small reed huts spread along the river bank; a herd of water buffalo lay wallowing in the cool muddy water, completely submerged but for the nose and eyes, which followed us as we passed with a look of blissful unconcern. On shore, the women were weaving the pliable wispy reeds into mats. Thousands of mats were stacked in large piles just outside the village, waiting for their river journey by raft to the market. But the still, stagnant waters throughout these marshes were notorious for bilharzia, and so we decided not to stop. The thought of having to wade through the oozing mud outweighed our curiosity.

At latitude 31° 9.5′ North, longitude 47° 26′ East, we came within the bounds of Admiralty Chart number 3847, the first chart of the Tigris river. But the chart had been published in 1938, for the first and last time, with no subsequent corrections. The more we studied the chart and our surroundings, the more confused the picture became. In some places it marked a conspicuous clump of palm trees where, in reality, there was nothing but palm trees for as far as the eye could see. It was really useless. We soon gave up trying to navigate with it and proceeded by our own methods which we had used for the last 700 miles.

As the sun began to set, we pulled into the reeds for the night. We were just settling down to cook a scratch meal from our meagre rations when we heard a rustling. Someone or something was coming through the reeds towards us. Always uncertain of our reception in a new area, we slowly reached into the port locker for our Turkish knives. The reeds parted. Peering out, wide-eyed, was a small and very frightened Arab who badly needed a shave. Replacing our knives, we gave a friendly sign of greeting, placing our right hands across our hearts, whereupon our visitor became more relaxed and even managed a wan smile. He pointed upstream, where we could just make out a wisp of smoke drifting lazily upwards from the reed tops; he pointed at us and again at the smoke, and disappeared back into the reeds.

We motored back upstream for 100 yards until we noticed a dugout canoe half hidden in the reeds, and a narrow pathway leading inland. I came alongside and Dave threw the anchor ashore. Using the dug-out as a jetty, we made the shore without wading through the mud, and soon came to a clearing half occupied by a reed hut. Our reception was a mixed one. The wife, clothed in a long black yashmak, continued laying mats down on the hard-packed earth in modest Muslim manner; a young son aged about 10 came forward to do the honours, accompanied by another boy just able to walk, his face covered in sores. As soon as he caught sight of two strange white men, the latter let out a shrill cry and scuttled off inside the hut, shrieking at the top of his voice.

The hut was made of thick bamboo-type reeds, covered with heavy woven green mats, spread over an area approximately the same as a double garage. Our host re-appeared and asked us to be seated while his wife produced a pile of unleavened bread and a bowl of sour milk. A single oil lamp was suspended from a pole to one side of us, so that shadows of moths, mosquitoes and other insects, attracted by the light, danced around the walls of our reed barricade. As we began to eat, the acrid smoke from burning camel dung stung our eyes. Even in the dark gloom we could see how pitifully poor our surroundings were; in one corner was a large, crude communal wooden bed. Over the dirty straw mattress a mosquito net was draped, with holes large enough for a crow to enter. This was without doubt the poorest family we had come across to date, yet they still felt obliged to help feed two unknown travellers. I felt guilty at taking their food when we had more than they had ever seen aboard *Hermes*.

More depressing still was the topic of our conversation, conducted mainly by sign language; they still regarded Britain as a leading world power, and talked continuously of sending their elder son to London to be educated, a hope, a dream they desperately clung to. Not knowing quite how to react, we chewed away at the hard dry bread, nodded our approval, but gently refused their persistent offers of more. The husband sensed that we were finding this a little difficult to chew and went off to find a bowl of dates. They insisted that we should eat them. They were now giving us all they had, even their most prized delicacy, and we could not refuse for fear of causing offence.

When the tea was made, I saw that our chance had come at last. The rusty sugar tin was empty; I looked across at Dave, who nodded and went down to *Hermes*, returning with a large bag of sugar. Their look of appreciation was a wonderful sight. The woman served the tea, replaced the pot and stepped back; suddenly she gave a startled cry, and in one swift movement stooped down, picked up a small stone and began to beat hard at something running across one of the mats. The small creature, three inches long, lay stunned on the ground; it gave a last snap of its claws, a flick of its deadly tail and lay still. The woman threw the dead scorpion into the reeds and sat down as though nothing had happened.

We soon returned to *Hermes* to retire for the night, relieved to have the safety of the water surrounding us. Early the next morning, after breakfasting with our friends on bread and tea, we set off once more, hoping to make Basra by nightfall. By the village of Qurnah, at the confluence of the Tigris and the Euphrates, we saw the famous apple tree, surrounded by a high circular wall. A notice informed us in both Arabic and English that 'On this holy spot where Tigris meets Euphrates this holy tree of our father Adam grew. Symbolising the Garden of Eden on earth, Abraham prayed here 2000 BC' Although the traditional site of the Garden of Eden lies over 400 miles to the north-west, between Baghdad and Habbaniyah, thousands of Muslim Arabs come to this spot every year on a pilgrimage.

Below Qurnah the river is known as the Shat-al-Arab, and flows, after 200 miles, directly into the Persian Gulf. Basra, fifty miles to the south, was to be our last port of call in Iraq; my plan was to obtain customs clearance from here and do a direct passage into the Gulf and across to Kuwait. In Basra, the only international trading port of Iraq, we saw ships of 10,000–15,000 tons, most of them Russian, moored in the river and alongside large quays and jetties.

We stayed as guests of the Basra Petroleum Company for three days, spending our time going through the painstakingly slow formalities of obtaining our clearance.

On the afternoon of our departure, we left *Hermes* alongside a jetty while we cleared up the last of the paperwork on shore. It was almost dark before we returned, and I decided to motor a few miles downstream before anchoring for the night. *Hermes* responded well enough to the helm. When we found a suitable spot, Dave went forward ready to throw the anchor overboard. The peaceful evening air was suddenly rent asunder by a string of blasphemous oaths, which made my heart miss a few beats. 'The whole bloody stem has come away,' he cried. I reached for the torch and scanned *Hermes*' port and starboard sides. There was no doubt about it: the whole portside was badly smashed in. My spirits sank to rock bottom—this was the end.

'Oh, my God,' I exclaimed, 'she's a bloody wreck.' I slumped forward in despair; we had done the Tigris, we had survived the rapids and shallows, sickness and the heat. Now with only one third of our total travelling distance behind us some bastard had bashed into us and the voyage was finished.

9

I SAT DOWN IN A DAZE, after standing to shout another volley of obscenities. Obviously one of the small ferries approaching Basra jetty must
have used *Hermes* as a fender. But now what? To pack it in was unthinkable. But we had only one day left on our visas. Officially we had already
left Iraq. We would have to repair her as best we could in the morning, to
make her seaworthy enough at least to cross the head of the Persian Gulf
and into Kuwait. There was nothing we could do that night. I lay down
uneasily, still cursing the ineptitude of ferry captains, and slept fitfully.

At first light I inspected the damage more thoroughly. Much of the port
side would need replanking. With the stemhead ripped away, the forestays
were only fixed onto a thin piece of wood. All we could do for the moment
was to try to make some sort of temporary repair, by tacking strips of canvas along the port side and making it waterproof with a liberal coating of
yellow paint. I hoped that in Kuwait we might find a decently equipped
workshop where I could carry out more effective repairs, which would enable us to reach Bahrain. I felt uneasy at going on towards the Persian Gulf
with *Hermes* in such an unseaworthy condition, but Dave agreed with me
that it was a calculated risk that we should take.

Twenty miles south of Basra the Shat-al-Arab becomes the no-man's-
land between Iraq and Iran; for many years a political conflict had existed
between the two countries over the ownership of the river. We decided to
stay on the Iraqi side as we were now experienced at dealing with Iraqi red
tape. Amongst the tall green reeds along the Iraqi bank we began to notice
peculiar clumps of dead withered grass, growing in the strangest way with
some of its roots uppermost. When I stood up in *Hermes* and waved at one
of these yellow clumps of weird plant life, two heads popped up, followed
by the rest of two soldiers in camouflage. They stood looking stupidly at
us as we went past, undecided whether to shoot or wave back. Fortunately

112

for us they chose to wave.

Fao, an oil terminal at the mouth of the Shat-al-Arab, drifted by to starboard. Accompanied by a dozen or more dhows, we entered the Persian Gulf, and unfolded our last chart, which would take us as far as Bahrain. As I was drawing in a course for Kuwait, I remembered the last time I had looked at this chart, back at home in Emsworth. I remembered wondering at the time whether it would ever be used. To arrive in the Persian Gulf meant that we were past the point of no return. Ahead of us was a direct sea route to Australia: no more land travel or difficult rivers to bar our passage, just sea, 8000 miles of it. Behind us lay the part of the voyage that would leave its mark on our minds for as long as we lived; the heat, disease and hardships over the past six weeks we would never forget.

For ten hours the motor droned unceasingly, pushing the crippled *Hermes* at 4½ knots through an oily smooth sea. At nightfall the lights of Kuwait cast an orange glow over the murky waters of its harbour. We wandered down the lines of shipping—oil tankers, cargo vessels and passenger ships—until we came to a small boat basin, and found an unoccupied jetty. Within minutes the customs officials arrived to search us for liquor; thanks to prohibition, a bottle of whisky would fetch anything up to £15 on the black market. Satisfied that we were a dry ship, they took me off to the main customs and immigration office to deal with our entry permits, an operation that lasted until the early hours of the morning.

Five exhausting, weary days followed in the blistering heat of Kuwait, as we tried to get money sent out from England and repairs effected on *Hermes*. We failed miserably on both counts; the money never came, and we could find no plywood for the repairs. We both felt at a very low ebb. But we received a visitor, in the shape of an official from the British Embassy, a tall, distinguished gentleman with a colonel's moustache. He looked down on us from his lofty perch high on the wall, and enquired, in a rather haughty tone, if we happened to be Messrs Pyle and Derrick. After we had produced proof of our identification, he explained that we had been lost without trace by my father in England. 'Well, I see you are still alive, anyway,' he said-and sauntered off, with his mind set at rest.

With our last dinars in my pocket, I went off to Cable and Wireless to send my father a telegram. By now our finances, mainly due to thieving, were past the acutely desperate stage—they just did not exist. Our food stocks were almost as low, although more was waiting for us at Bahrain. But that was still 200 miles away. There was only one hope left, to see if we could thumb a lift on one of the ships in dock that was bound for Bahrain. It went entirely against the grain, but it was the only course open to us. 'There is no other way, Dave, we've got to get a lift somehow,' I said as I poured the last packet of Chicken Bombay into the saucepan. Dave looked solemnly at the dark brown powder fusing with the water.

'Yes, I know, but it just doesn't seem right.'

'I couldn't agree with you more, but we have no alternative.'

We spent our sixth day in Kuwait visiting every ship we could find, British, French, Indian, Russian, Romanian, Greek, German, any ship that might be going our way.

Every time we drew a blank, except at one of the British India Steamship Company's line. They could not take us themselves, but the first officer gave us an introduction to the captain of their sister ship, the SS *Dwarka*, due in two days' time, and bound for Bahrain. We were just reconciling ourselves to the thought of two days without food, after subsisting on the barest of rations for the past three days, when we picked up the fascinating titbit of information that the local hospital paid £12 for a pint of blood. Within half an hour we were both lying prostrate in the hospital, eagerly watching the small polythene bags as they slowly filled with our dark red, disease-ridden blood. After a quick, ice-cold orange drink, we raced to the cashier's desk, to start counting our money. It felt like some ultra-respectable form of prostitution; but we consoled ourselves with the thought that at least our bellies would be full that night. To celebrate our new affluence, we went to a small restaurant in one of the bazaars and ate a huge meal of mutton and rice, washed down by a bottle of Coca-Cola and concluded by our belching in unison.

Early in the morning of the eighth day, we went down to the docks in eager anticipation. To our delight the *Dwarka* was anchored a few hundred yards off the main jetty. A launch pulled away from her side and came towards us; in the bows stood a white man in European clothing, who later introduced himself to us as Pete Farrel, captain of the *Dwarka*. When I handed him our introduction note, he glanced at it briefly. 'O.K., I'll take you.' Within two hours of our meeting Pete, *Hermes* was on board *Dwarka*, and we were drinking tea in one of her cabins. I began to feel somewhat ashamed of having this lift, but I could think of no other way out. To sail with *Hermes* in her present condition, for 200 miles to Bahrain, could spell disaster for both her and her crew. Now at last we could relax, and within twenty-four hours we would be under the care of the RAF in Bahrain. *Hermes* could be repaired and thoroughly overhauled ready to sail the 8000 miles to Australia.

When *Dwarka* nosed her way next day through the crystal clear waters of Bahrain harbour, the sparkling, vivid blues, reds and whites of coral patches were running close along her side. As her black and white hull glided up to the dock, lines were thrown ashore and the heavy warps were hauled in by the dock workers. His work over for a few hours, Pete invited us to his cabin for a farewell drink, while the RAF were notified of our arrival, and *Hermes* was being hoisted off by *Dwarka*'s derricks and transported to the customs compound. Dave and I were both out of training; after an hour at Pete's cocktail cabinet, we were more than slightly inebriated. There was a knock at the door, and within a few seconds, Squadron Leader Gerry Holmes was also sitting in a chair, clutching a glass of ice-cold beer. Another hour passed, by which time Gerry, Dave and myself, had become the best of drinking companions. The sun had set before we staggered down the gangway and stumbled towards Gerry's house.

We tried to begin work on *Hermes* the following day. It was Friday, the Muslim equivalent of our Sunday, and so the customs compound was closed. Saturday was recovery day from Friday, and Sunday was the Christian holiday, so it wasn't until Monday that we managed to drag *Hermes* out of the compound and down to the Joint Services Yacht Club at HMS *Jufair*. This was the naval headquarters in Bahrain, and we hoped that with the brotherhood of the sea, the navy would come to our help. A maintenance craft lay nearby, where a number of naval shipwrights were employed. I noticed they had vast stacks of plywood, mechanical band saws, circular saws and planers in the workshop; a few days of hard work with this equipment, and we could soon have *Hermes* seaworthy once more.

The sailing club grounds were deserted. As soon as Gerry had found a clear space, Dave and I set to work cleaning her out. Gerry had alerted the navy that we wanted help, and later that morning two naval commanders strolled over towards us. Naturally we stopped what we were doing, expecting them to speak. But they ignored us. Standing six feet away, they stared diffidently at *Hermes*. Having surveyed the damaged port side for five minutes, one of them drew himself up to his full height. 'In my professional opinion,' he drawled, 'I just do not think it can be done.' The other nodded in agreement.

'Too right, old man. Speaking for myself, I wouldn't even cross the harbour in this.' They looked at one another and nodded once more. Tweedledum and Tweedledee then walked away.

We allowed them a few yards grace before giving them, free, gratis and for nothing, our professional opinion of their ancestry. 'Why don't you get in some sea time...' Tempers are quickly frayed in the summer heat of the Persian Gulf.

From my previous experience with the services, I had found it better to approach the 'other ranks', the men on the shop floor, when in need of help or advice. We explained that we were only too happy to do the work ourselves, but that our tools were limited and unsuitable for such a major reconstruction. The petty officers and shipwright ratings quickly rallied to our rescue; after Gerry had found a few sheets of plywood, they cut it up into shape for us and loaned us some tools. Five days after our arrival in Bahrain, work began at last, and continued for a further seven days until *Hermes* was totally transformed from a near total wreck into her buoyant self once more.

Gerry Holmes found us a bungalow for the duration, and we were made guests of the Officers' Mess, fortunately frequented only by the air force and army. There was no great hurry to leave—we could not venture out into the Arabian Sea until the south-west monsoon had finished at the end of October. Life became a round of frivolous gaiety; the food was magnificent, whisky was available at fifteen shillings a bottle, bathing on the sheikh's warm sandy beaches was free. Everything that a carefree bachelor could possibly desire, in fact, with one exception. We were both given free medical and dental attention, and slowly our bodies filled out to their natural shapes, and our strength returned.

By the time we were ready for sea once more, the transmitter had been overhauled by the RAF; radio schedules with the army at Bahrain and the RAF at Sharjah would give us greater safety in crossing the 350 miles of the Gulf to Dubai. The water tanks were filled to their maximum capacity of twenty-eight gallons, which, according to the RAF survival booklet, would be sufficient for four days' supply for two persons in the Persian Gulf during the summer. This meant that we would probably have to take on more water before Dubai, but we were assured by the RAF that on the island of Halul, sixty miles south-east of the northern tip of Qatar, there was an American oil company and that water was available there.

Early in the morning of 6 October, we sailed out of Bahrain and laid a course for the barren, reef-strewn northern headland of Qatar.

The day was already stiflingly hot with the sun beating down onto the glassy smooth sea. 'twenty-eight gallons of water, four days' supply'; this thought kept running through my mind. 'What if the outboard motor packs up?' 'What if we have no wind?' 'What if the transmitter breaks down?' There were so many ifs, a situation that I hated and feared.

The odd Arab trading dhow passed by, their crew giving us friendly waves. Ahead of us a strange illusion began to appear—clumps of palm trees hung high in the air; as we approached, their stems seemed to stretch downwards and their tops seemed to rise still higher until they appeared to be a thousand feet tall—until suddenly they vanished. We had often seen smaller mirages, but this was fantastic.

At least three hours passed before we spotted the real trees off the starboard bow, reaching out to the headland of Qatar. According to the chart, a coral reef extended up to three miles offshore, but since many of the trading dhows were motoring over it, we decided to do the same. The water was crystal clear; numerous passages could easily be spotted through the rainbow-coloured patches of coral, but many ended abruptly in a reef covered by only a few inches of water, too shallow even for *Hermes*. The sun began to set over the desert of Qatar and, since piloting through these reefs in darkness would be highly dangerous, we slowly weaved our way seaward into deeper water.

After motoring for over twelve hours our fuel was running short, so I decided to head directly for Halul island. It seemed as though we were going to be plagued continuously by having no wind, as we now were. Water was our biggest problem; to be without water in the Persian Gulf in the summer spells a quick but very painful death. With virtually no shade from the sun, and the glare and heat of it reflecting from the smooth glassy sea, our consumption rose to 3½ gallons per man per day. Conditions were vastly different from what I had experienced in the North Atlantic, where two pints per day were sufficient for survival. As a safety precaution we carried lashed to the liferaft four Solar stills, six desalting kits and 2½ gallons of canned wate. Even so, if ever we had to take to the raft, we would be lucky to survive three days, according to the survival booklet.

At 2100 hours that night we contacted the RAF. 'Bahrain to *Hermes*. Regret no fuel, no water at Halul island. Repeat, no fuel, no water at Halul Island.'

'Now they bloody well tell us!' I cursed, reaching for the chart of the Persian Gulf. Das Island was the only other place where we could obtain supplies—but this was a further 50 miles beyond Halul, out of our fuel range. I altered course for Das, and we motored on through the still warm night, our precious fuel burning away into useless carbon monoxide.

Early the following morning the motor spluttered to a halt, with Das Island still over 30 miles away to the south-east. Dave went forward to hoist the sails, a ritual that he had now brought down to fifteen seconds flat; but the sails just hung limp and parched in the morning sun. There was not a breath of wind to stir the warm sultry air. Admittedly we had a number of safety factors on our side, with the emergency rations and contact with Bahrain. But there was still an element of very real danger in our present predicament. At 0900 we contacted Bahrain again to inform them of our position; we still had over two days of water before having to broach our emergency rations.

Eighty miles to the west lay the barren sunbaked shores of the Trucial

Oman States and Saudi Arabia. At 1000 hours I looked up from the chart and gazed towards them. At first I thought the sun was causing a glow on the horizon, but after a few minutes I could see an orange haze forming; a sand-storm—wind. A short swell began to roll *Hermes* from side to side. Her masts slowly swayed across the translucent sky. I felt the welcome caress of a hot wind playing on my right cheek.

'It's wind, Dave, w-i-n-d!' The sails began to move, just a little at first, then slowly billowed into shape. *Hermes* heeled gently; ripples extended from her bow and formed a fine frothy wake which slipped by astern with a soft plopping sound as they lapped against the clinker hull. The wind had come. We were moving once more towards the oasis of Das island.

Within an hour a good breeze was coming in from the south-west; the haze thickened, and fine sand particles formed a gritty white coating on the decks until a wave washed them clean again. As the morning drifted into the afternoon thick, black smoke appeared over the horizon ahead. Then we saw orange flames licking the sky, and a low hump of land. The wind held, and by early evening we were entering the small harbour on the southern tip of Das Island. A few tugs and a cable-laying ship lay alongside the concrete walls. When a young chap on the cable ship waved to us, we sailed up alongside. Leaning over the side, he asked where we were from.

'England,' I shouted up.

'Ye must be focking mad. Come an' 'ave a beer.'

The sweetest words we had heard in a long while.

Cowering in the far corner of the small man-made harbour were three forty-foot Arab trading dhows, strangely out of place in this remote, all-male British community. Das, a mere dot in the centre of the Persian Gulf, is an island of only one square mile in size, a barren lump of rock and coral bleached white by the sun; yet 1200 British men lived and worked here, refining the oil from a complex of rigs out at sea and pumping it into the huge super-tankers which visited the island every few days. If the Arab dhows were out of place, even more so was the real English pub we visited later that evening, complete with genuine barrels of genuine English beer. This strange island was an oasis surrounded by water, but a true oasis all the same.

David and I were loading our supplies on board the following morning when a group of well-wishers arrived with a supply of beer. Boxes of cigars, souvenir flags and wooden shields were handed over as each one shook us by the hand and wished us good luck for the journey that lay ahead. As we drifted out through the harbour entrance, our friend from the cable ship leaned down from the harbour wall. 'I still think you're bloody mad, but good luck!' Our stay had been so brief, yet the hospitality had been overwhelming.

As we set course for Dubai, the setting sun cast an orange glow over the little island; thick black smoke rose into the air from the refinery at its northern end. But unusual atmospheric conditions prevented us from establishing radio contact with either Bahrain or Sharjah at the scheduled time of 2100 hours. Once more we had been cut off in a miniature world of our own, just two men in a very small boat, a very long way from home. We started the motor. *Hermes* had just started to pick up speed, her bows cutting through the black sea, when out of the gloom ahead a weird three-legged monster suddenly appeared. We could hear the sea swirling around its legs. I altered course to port and we slipped close by a great round iron leg, one of three supporting a derelict oil rig. Once we had passed, it stood out in a huge ghostly silhouette against the glowing background of Das Island.

The following day was hot and oppressive. The sun blazed down and bounced back at us off the shimmering sea. Not a whisper of cool wind came along and we lay sweltering, occasionally reaching for the canvas water bags which normally hung, perspiring, on the mizzen mast. In the early afternoon we sighted the barren, sandy island of Sir Abu Nu'ayr, which is totally devoid of any vegetation. A most inhospitable place. Again we had to use the motor before our water supply became too low.

We were both experiencing a loneliness that we had not known before. When life is balanced on such finely adjusted scales, when the possibility of a painful death from thirst is so close, life takes on a new meaning. The Mediterranean was like a motorway, by comparison. It offered beautiful scenery, but no fear of the unknown. The Tigris was full of hardship; the rapids, the shallows and fear of disease represented a challenge which needed brute force and strong nerves to surmount. Here in the Persian Gulf, past the point of no return, I felt a long way from the safety of home. There was no turning back now. The unknown was out there ahead, waiting for us. It is at times like this, faced by the unknown, that the human body can endure more than is often thought possible. The urge to live is supreme and overpowering.

It is at times like this, too, that thoughts turn with increasing frequency to the supernatural, to the power that guides us all. I cannot speak for the other Dave, because he was an agnostic, and we deliberately avoided the subject. Although I had never been attracted as a youngster to the trappings of organised religion, nevertheless I shared with most—if not all—sailors a profound respect for the basic truths of Christianity. Indeed I would be very surprised indeed if anyone who had experienced the fears and the sorrows and the discomforts that we had endured should subsequently turn around and deny the existence of God. I would never do so: I have had too many of my prayers answered. It would be ungrateful, to say the least. Perhaps this applies particularly to the skipper. After all, the final decision is the skipper's; he can be a very lonely man indeed unless he can call upon someone for help and guidance, someone to share the burden of responsibility.

I switched on at the appointed time and began to call up RAF Bahrain. For ten long minutes I sent out a continuous call, but only received an earful of static. We were in no immediate danger, but we felt a desperate need to hear an English voice, to establish contact with someone in the outside world. We almost willed a voice to come through. Eventually, with blessed relief, we made contact with RAF Sharjah, whose radio operator had heard us repeatedly calling Bahrain, and had decided to establish contact himself. I had to restrain myself from audibly throwing my arms around his neck. Instead, with true stiff upper lip I gave him our position and ETA for Dubai. While off watch that night I slept soundly without a care in the world.

We dared not risk leaving the Persian Gulf just yet, because of the gales in the Arabian Sea. Fierce south-west monsoon winds, which blow uninterrupted from the Indian Ocean, sweep into the Arabian Sea from April until early October, and we had to wait for the gentle dry winds of the north-east monsoon from Iran, West Pakistan and India, which blow from October to the end of March. Although it was now mid-October, there was still the occasional report of a south-westerly gale in the Arabian Sea. This timing was critical as winter was approaching in the Persian Gulf, and winter brings the strong northerly *shamal* winds, often reaching storm force.

I spent many hours at the meteorological office at RAF Sharjah studying satellite weather photographs, waiting for the weather to improve. At last, on the afternoon of 21 October, we had a favourable report. The south-westerly monsoon had receded far enough to the south in the Arabian Sea to enable us to proceed onwards to Karachi.

22ND OCTOBER 1969 DEPARTED 1630 HOURS FROM SERVICES YACHT CLUB. WIND N.W. FORCE 5 SEA STATE MODERATE TEMPERATURE 110°F.

A thousand miles of unwelcoming sea lay ahead of us before we were to reach Karachi. The coastline of Muscat, South Iran and West Pakistan had little to offer in the way of refuge. Back in England I had been warned of this coastline by Jed Lavery, a BOAC captain who had often flown high above this coast. 'It's about the most barren and inhospitable area I have ever seen,' he informed me one evening a few days before we were due to leave. Now we were about to see it for ourselves. His words echoed in my thoughts as we set the sails and headed north-eastwards along the Trucial Oman coast.

Our gateway from the Persian Gulf into the Gulf of Oman and the Arabian Sea was through the narrow Hormuz Strait, with Iran to one side and the States of Muscat and Oman to the other. As we approached the precipitous cliffs of Muscat's headland, the seas began to teem with life. Never had we seen so many black-and-yellow-banded sea snakes weaving their way across the smooth surface of the water. Their heads projected two or three inches above the sea, like a mass of miniature Loch Ness monsters. Porpoises, dolphins and barracuda leaped and dived around us. A giant Manta ray with its eight-foot wing span leaped high into the air only ten yards off and slammed down on the surface with stunning velocity, a sight seen by many mariners and still not fully understood. Maybe it was to free itself from the irritation of sea lice, or to stun a shoal of smaller fish, after which it would glide around at leisure close to the surface collecting its supper. I was rather proud of my new fishing line that I had bought at Sharjah and had it trailing over the stern. With the amazing sights all around I had forgotten all about it until I heard a sudden twang. I hauled it in smartly, to find a large, ugly fish's head with its jaws fastened around the hook, but nothing else. A barracuda or a shark must have taken the meatier portion. Nervously I edged my way farther into the boat, having no great wish to come into close contact with any of those fellows.

A few days after leaving Dubai we were crossing the Gulf of Oman, heading towards the southern shores of Iran and West Pakistan. Sailing at night along this formidable coastline was eerie and strange: not a single light flickered from the dark mountainous shores. A strange stillness enveloped our small world; all was still except for the occasional swish where some creature from the depths had broken the surface. The sea contained the only life; the shores were barren, inhospitable, lifeless, dry—as though from another planet. Since there was no moon, and the sea was as black as Indian ink, helming became a test of nerves; a sudden loud snort and swirl of water would quicken the heart beat and send a cold shiver through the body, despite the warm night air.

During one night, 300 miles west of Karachi, we saw ahead of us a seething, boiling cauldron. Yet the sea was calm all round, except for a long swell running in from the south. It was the 'sea of fire', according to the pilot guide of the North Arabian Sea, a phenomenon often seen by mariners of the past; an area of brilliant phosphorescence alive with glowing plankton and other small sea creatures. Soon after we had sailed through this strange phenomenon a dozen or more glowing discs, three or four feet across, glided beneath our keel. Numerous pairs of large glowing eyes swept around us just below the surface. The discs were probably turtles swimming ashore, towards a small sandy cove where they could lay their eggs. As for the eyes, I am still baffled.

The nights were frightening. At two o'clock one morning, we were joined by two large dolphins almost as long as the boat; bathed in phosphorescence, they gracefully swam around us for over half an hour, before returning to join the other spirits of the deep. Our oceans cover two-thirds of the world's surface, and yet so little is known of their contents; this part of the Arabian Sea, which few can have seen in the way we were seeing it, must hold some fascinating material beneath its surface.

We were working our way as quickly as we could along the coast towards Karachi; but from Dubai it was a run of almost 1000 miles, and our water was getting low. I was even more alarmed when, in a choppy sea, the aerial suddenly broke in two. Admittedly we had lost contact with the RAF by this time, but I felt uneasy that we were no longer able to transmit. The wind held fine, blowing a moderate breeze from the south-west, and a hundred miles west of Karachi there was the small fishing village of Ormara, situated on a narrow rocky isthmus jutting out into the Arabian Sea. If our water supply became desperately short we could call in there and refill our tanks.

A few Arabian dhows, a beautiful sight under full sail, overtook us to seaward. They were plying their cargo of Persian carpets, spices and probably a few bars of gold from the Persian Gulf to Pakistan and India. The smuggling of gold is rife in these parts; in the last twenty years the naval patrol vessels have caught hundreds of dhows with tens of thousands of pounds' worth of gold on board. Thanks to these patrols, to take it by sea was now a risky business; a new smuggling route had been opened up by establishing a camel train through the desert fifty miles north of the coastline. As yet, the police had not been able to catch this band; according to the smugglers, their camels were specially trained for high-speed performance.

Since the south-west monsoon had finished only a week or two before, we were expecting the occasional strong blow, and it came. Twenty miles west of Ormara heavy thunderous clouds formed, stretching the entire length of the horizon to the south. A sea began to run in, increasing steadily in size as the night drew on. The wind followed, whipping the crests of the waves off and sending the spray suddenly into the troughs. The night was pitch black, with an occasional flicker of lightning far out to sea, picking out the rocky headland of Ormara. *Hermes* rode every wave with ease, scudding down their faces, her bow cleaving its way through the dark waters.

Dave lowered the main with practised ease, while I worked out a course to clear the rocky headland's eastern point and to come in under its lee. From the dark void ahead we suddenly heard a frightened call. We could see nothing except the white froth of the wave tops tumbling before us. Then, a hundred yards off the starboard bow, there was the faint flicker of a light. Sitting there, totally unconcerned at the raging sea around him, was an old man dressed in a white dhoti, fishing from a small dug-out canoe. As we passed close to his little craft, I gave him a wave. 'Good evening,' I called out. (How else can one greet an old man out fishing in a near gale?) I felt almost ashamed at running for shelter; but I will always stick to my own convictions and do what I think is sensible. As we rounded the headland, the seas calmed and we sailed into a bay.

The wind was now blowing across to us direct from the village of Ormara, and a strong smell of rotting fish made our nostrils twitch. There were still no lights to be seen, but the roar of the sea breaking on a beach not far ahead indicated that we had arrived off the village. Dave went forward to drop the anchor. We had reached Pakistan.

We awoke at dawn to find ourselves covered in a thin layer of fine, powdery dust. The wind was blowing more strongly than during the night, and was now coming directly from the west, blowing along the desert coastline and carrying before it a dense cloud of fine sand. We were lying 300 yards off shore, sheltered by the village of Ormara, and a crowd of men, women and children had gathered on the sandy beach, looking out towards us and talking excitedly. I waved and called out a friendly 'hullo', which they seemed to find rather amusing. We ran in towards the beach, under power, but a large swell was running in on to the sands. When we were 100 yards off, I indicated to Dave to drop anchor again. We slowly paid out the anchor warp and drifted in towards the beach, making her fast just outside the breaking surf. I dived over the side and swam towards the shore, travelling the last fifty yards in a welter of foam and frothing water.

The sight of a half-naked, exhausted, bedraggled Englishman picking himself up off the sand after being cast ashore like a shipwrecked mariner was evidently hilarious for these cheerful Pakistanis. A number came down to help me up the beach and shook my hand, speaking some strange words of greeting. I was escorted up the long beach towards a large group of wood and mud houses. Walking through the village I soon discovered the source of the smell we had experienced earlier. In the village centre lay an acre of ground almost entirely covered by a large, very old and very dirty canvas awning. Underneath were a number of deep pits, ten feet square, dug into the sandy soil. A dozen men sat around these holes, gutting large quantities of fish, splitting them open and laying them on top of one another in the pits, then filling it in with sackfuls of salt. A pack of thin, mangy-looking dogs wandered around the men as they worked, greedily snapping up the fish innards. We had been wandering through the Middle East for some time now, and I had seen many more unpleasant sights. This was the life that had been led for many hundreds of years, and so who was I to question that?

I was shown to the local police officer's house, a white mud and stone building with a small earth-covered yard, where he washed, ate and slept. He had been sent to the village from Karachi three years ago, and seemed to like his trouble-free existence in this friendly village. The formalities were minimal, which made a pleasant change. I was offered tea, served for the first time in the Middle East with milk, but the mixture tasted strongly saline. He spoke excellent English and so I asked him about this. 'It has not rained here significantly for the past twelve years. Our only water supply is a well, and as we are so close to the sea, it is bound to taste brackish,' he told me. I tried some water straight from a sweating earthenware jar. It tasted strongly of salt; no matter how much I drank, I found I was still thirsty. So we had a problem. We had come here for fresh water, apart from seeking shelter from the gale. I had an uneasy feeling that the next few days were not going to be too pleasant if all we could drink was a liquid which tasted pretty much the same as sea water.

In fact we spent three days in Ormara, waiting for the gale to abate. By experimenting with various types and strengths of tea and coffee, the water ceased to be quite so unpalatable, and the villagers showed a great warmth of human kindness and hospitality. Ormara was a village almost forgotten by the rest of West Pakistan. A supply boat from Karachi occasionally came with rice and vegetables, but when it was due to arrive next no one knew; for the past six months they had managed without their rice and their vegetables. They lived solely on fish and an occasional egg, when one of the scrawny chickens decided to lay.

It was with some sadness that we finally left this wonderful little community. The following evening, the loom of the lighthouse at Karachi swept a dull glow over the horizon; we had made good time on the last 100 miles. By mid-morning of 3 November we were motoring past the breakwater and into the teeming harbour of the capital port of West Pakistan.

10

W E MOTORED PAST THE VAST, RUST-STAINED HULKS of 10,000 to 15,000-ton cargo-ships, moored along jetties that stretched as far as the eye could see. Down the line we noticed the black and white funnel of a British India steamship, with a few lighters lying alongside helping to off-load the cargo, like a sow with a litter of piglets. A young British officer, dressed in white tropical kit, stood close by the bridge directing operations. He waved to us and came running down the gangway to the lower deck. 'We've been told to look out for you,' he shouted between cupped hands. 'Tie up alongside the lighter and come aboard.'

Once we were installed in the officers' bar, Dave and I got down to some serious drinking to make up for lost time. After half an hour or so a smartly dressed Pakistani joined us. He introduced himself as Pesi Sorab, secretary of the Karachi Yacht Club. 'I asked the British India Company to look out for you and inform me on your arrival.' In fact Pesi turned out to be British, and was out in Karachi for a couple of years to run the computer section of a large bank. After a few more drinks in the bar, we became the best of friends and Pesi insisted that we should both come and stay with him and his wife for as long as we were in Karachi.

Karachi is the only commercial port of any significance in West Pakistan; although not the capital, it is the centre of the commercial trade of the country. Hundreds of thousands of villagers from the desert wastelands to the north come into Karachi for work, living in squalid shanty towns surrounding the city. But as we drove towards Pesi's bungalow, I noticed large, Victorian-style houses of the British Raj period cheek by jowl with ultra-modern flats and offices. To the north, where we were heading, there were vast expanses of barren sandy desert where large estates of modern luxurious bungalows were being built, producing an open-plan city sprawled out over many tens of square miles. Karachi may have

Malaysian fish trap in the Malacca Straits

Proa dug-out on the shore, covered with palm leaves to stop it cracking up in the heat

Selling live fish in Chinatown, Singapore

The market place, Chinatown, Singapore

little to offer in the way of beauty, but because of the friendliness and pride of the Pakistanis, it is a place I came to love.

We moved into Pesi's luxurious bungalow, which had a large tiled patio in the centre and air-conditioned rooms leading off all round. The two houseboys and gardener were quartered in a small building behind; his chauffeur and gate man lived elsewhere in the city. Pesi's English wife, Celia, came out of one of the bedrooms and walked across the patio towards us. 'Welcome to Karachi. I've made up a couple of beds in Adam's room—he's our son. Both he and our daughter, Zerena, are still at school, but should be back later this afternoon.' Celia showed us into a large bedroom with pictures of planes, boats and cars plastered all over the walls. A door leading off from the far side opened into a separate bathroom. The bedroom, like the rest of the bungalow, was furnished with ultramodern western furniture, very comfortable and very expensive.

We spent most of our first three days meeting the British community, either at the sailing club, or at the British Club, which was an impressive, mock-Victorian mansion, whose rooms were decorated with old portraits of formidable brigadiers and generals, sporting huge handlebar moustaches. Although the British were kind and hospitable, we were really much more anxious to meet the Pakistanis. One such was Zani, a young Pakistani girl secretary, who had spent the past few years travelling throughout America and Europe. Dave went off with Pesi one evening, leaving me with the privilege of taking Zani out to dinner. She picked me up at Pesi's bungalow and drove me in her old Renault Dauphine down to a beach, a mile eastward of Karachi harbour, flanked by a promenade, half a mile long, paved with large reddish-brown flagstones. Another paved pathway led down to the beach, an avenue of shrubs and trees that was broken up by a series of granite and marble statues. 'This is where the British ladies used to take their Sunday walks,' she announced. 'No one else was allowed to set foot here, except the gardeners and servants.' We left the car where horse carriages had once stopped and strolled down the promenade. Stall holders were selling lemonade and peanuts, where once the servants had waited patiently for their mistresses to return; the long walk towards the beach was now crowded with Pakistani families; hordes of ragged children were playing in the neglected shrubbery.

'So you don't think much of the British?'

'They brought their own little bit of England out here, and we were just their servants. Servants and slaves in our own country.'

'Let's go back and have some dinner,' I suggested.

The restaurant was clean, but not expensive; cheap metal tables, covered with disposable tablecloths, were scattered at random around the gaily lit room.

'Do you mind eating with your hands?' she asked.

'Not at all. I'm used to it.'

'What would you like to eat?' she asked.

'I'll leave that to you. I'll eat anything. And enjoy it!'

With Zani I began to understand the feelings of the Pakistani people. Sitting opposite me, she was overpoweringly attractive, dressed in her white cotton shalrvar trousers, the high-collared hameez jacket and long silk scarf, or dupatta. As we began to eat our rice, roast lamb and chapatis, I realised that she held strong views about the British. 'They always keep themselves to themselves, never mixing to the extent that we would like them to. No wonder they don't understand us!' She was getting into her stride, so I kept quiet. 'Like most people in the Middle and Far East, we are proud of our country, and don't like to be treated as inferiors. The Americans are better, but are so patronising, with their gifts and their kind words. But at least they try to help!'

'Hey, wait a minute,' I said. 'You're just as bad. At the old British Club and the Yacht Club, I've seen with my own eyes how many of your own people snub each other.'

'Those are the Anglicised ones,' she retorted disparagingly, 'the ones who always sidle up to the British or Americans, trying to gain favour. They are detestable. Worse than the British.'

'Please don't think that we're all like that,' I said. 'I'm sure that most British people nowadays wish Pakistan the very best.'

'I would believe that if I met a few more like you, who conform a bit more when here.'

'How do you mean?'

'Well—eat with their hands, for a start. Not trying to inflict their culture in a country that already has a very old and perfectly good culture of its own. Mixing readily with the people of our country.'

We argued on late into the evening. I found myself fighting a losing battle as I tried to establish the British people as an acceptable race.

'Anyway, Zani,' I said as I passed over 20 rupees to the waiter,' *I* understand your people. I'm sure many other British people do, too.'

'I know,' she said, looking up at me with a smile.

I saw Zani a few more times before we set sail for Bombay. On our last evening in Karachi, she invited Dave and myself to a dinner party at her home. Dave sat inside the house and ate with the family, while Zani and I wandered out into the garden with our plates full of curry. 'Will you be coming down to the Yacht Club to see us leave?' I asked as we savoured the cool evening air.

'No, it will spoil everything if I come over there—when will you be coming back to Karachi ?' she asked, looking straight at me with her beautiful large brown eyes.

'As soon as I possibly can,' I promised. And I meant it, too.

On 11 November we loaded *Hermes* up with fuel and fresh provisions. All our friends, with one exception, came down to the Yacht Club to wish us luck for the 600-mile trip to Bombay. I noticed that Maureen Allen, the wife of a British diplomat, was carrying an old biscuit tin and a wicker cat basket. 'Two apple pies for you,' she said. 'You also talked of having a cat on board, so I've brought one of the kittens we had at home. She's all yours—if you promise to look after her.'

I took the basket, unhooked the lid and peered inside. A little white and ginger face peered out at me and miaowed. 'She's lovely. Don't worry—we'll look after her!' Our third crew member was not more than five weeks old. As soon as we had cleared the harbour entrance, we opened her basket. Her little face poked out of her small wicker home, she raised her nose, gave two or three sniffs, and set up a long pathetic howl. 'She's frightened to hell, poor thing,' I said to Dave as I pulled her out and sat her on my lap. 'She's shaking like a leaf. Maybe we shouldn't have taken her.'

'She'll settle down eventually,' he said, as he guided *Hermes* southwards, taking a quick glance at the compass. 'I only hope she doesn't keep up that bloody noise all night.' I snuggled her close to me under my shirt, trying to calm her pathetic wail.

Later that evening, as we sailed southwards, down past the swampy shores of West Pakistan, she began to give vent once more to her feelings at being shanghaied. She refused to eat any of our dehydrated food and just howled. All night long she howled, walking precariously close to the gunwale, until we began to think that we had press-ganged a lousy sailor.

Three days after leaving Karachi, when we were about to cross the Gulf of Kutch, a strong north-westerly wind began to blow. As we sailed on, it increased to a full gale. Darkness came, and we still had not sighted the lights of the Indian port of Okha on the southern shores of the Gulf. To my alarm, a considerable amount of water began to swirl around the bilges and *Hermes* started to wallow in the swell. To make matters worse, the kitten's howls rose to a pitch, so that the sound grated on our nerves. 'As if we haven't enough trouble without her making that damned awful noise,' I yelled over the wind. The seas were now foaming at their tops and swirling past us on either side.

'Stuff her into one of the sleeping bags, Dave. Whatever you do, try and keep her quiet.'

'I'm trying to shut her up, but she's so petrified, I can't stop her.'

The water in the bilge increased, and we realised that *Hermes* was slowly sinking. At three o'clock in the morning I lifted up the bottom boards and found a spout of water shooting in aft of the centreboard casing.

I swallowed hard. We were breaking up; the strain of sailing over the past seven months, the overland journey to the upper reaches of the Tigris, the rapids and the smash up in the Shat-al-Arab, had all taken their toll. I brought *Hermes* round on an approximate course for the port of Okha where I hoped that with any luck we could beach her for repairs. If we lasted that long. As if she could read my thoughts, the kitten made several attempts to jump overboard, so we put her in a locker, where she began to howl even louder.

I looked at the chart of Port Okha, and noticed that it was surrounded by reefs; difficult to enter in calm weather, impossible in a gale. The light of the Port appeared on the bow, and we surfed towards it, the waves tumbling and cascading around us. Three miles off, still in pitch darkness, Dave threw out the sea anchor; we would have to wait until daylight.

What a night! One of us had to keep bailing continuously, desperately trying to stay afloat, while the other tried to get some rest with the kitten continuously wailing from inside the locker. At dawn we could see the waves smashing on to the reef, which formed a natural harbour breakwater. A mile to seaward I noticed a native fishing boat, with sails reefed, ploughing towards us. I decided to wait until she was abeam. I then followed her in through the narrow entrance, where the waves were tumbling over on top of one another in complete confusion. The last half mile into the harbour required every bit of skill and concentration I could muster, to prevent *Hermes* from broaching and rolling over, or smashing on the cruel jagged coral reef. Once we were inside the sea calmed down to a mere ripple and I ran her up on to a soft sandy beach close by a small naval establishment.

The inevitable crowd gathered on the beach as we started to clear the decks, ready to begin repairs. Three customs officials in white uniforms, barged their way through and appeared alongside. 'Where are you from?' one of them asked in perfect English.

'Karachi,' I replied.

'Why have you come here?'

'Because we were beginning to sink. I think the keel may be damaged.'

'I shall have to search jour boat,' he said, trying to sound very authoritative. Obviously he had never had to deal with a foreign boat before.

'Your privilege,' I replied.

India and Pakistan have never seen eye to eye since their independence in 1947. Anyone arriving from Pakistan falls under some suspicion, but due to our mode of travel, I had hoped for a slightly more hospitable welcome than this. While our customs friend was sorting through our equipment he became highly amused by the kitten, when her little white and ginger face poked out of one of the lockers. 'It's a Pakistani cat,' I said. The smile vanished and he began to search with renewed thoroughness.

Two young naval officers had come down meantime to see what was happening. One of them saw we had a radio transmitter and began to question me about it.

'What channels are you operating on?' I was tempted to tell him to get lost but thought better of it. 'What is your power output ?' 'What range?' I answered them all, and he seemed satisfied: his expression changed, and with a smile he invited us to dinner at their mess that evening.

The Customs began their search at ten o'clock in the morning, and finished it by mid-day; but it took us until four o'clock that afternoon, cursing all customs officers everywhere, to stow all the equipment back in the lockers and containers again. Meantime our little kitten had begun to settle down on shore and was scuttling around the sandy beach. But obviously *Hermes* was home. 'It's about time we gave her a name, don't you think?' I said to Dave as we watched her slowly creeping up on a small sand crab.

After discussing the subject for a while we decided unanimously that the most original and befitting name would be Eskimo Nell, or Nell for short. By this time it was too late to do any work on the keel, so we both had a quick bath in the sea before going along for dinner with the Indian Navy. Nell seemed content playing around on the sand and we were sure that she wouldn't wander far from *Hermes* while we were away. To our considerable surprise, our young friends had managed to procure two bottles of whisky, and we spent a cheerful evening discussing weather conditions within the Arabian Sea, the Indian Navy's role in the area as a base against West Pakistan and the smuggling of gold into India from the Persian Gulf. By midnight the two bottles had been demolished, the party broke up and we zigzagged back to *Hermes*, full of good will towards the Indian Navy.

At first light we began work on repairing *Hermes*. On close inspection I saw that the after section of the centreboard casing had pulled away from the keel and some of the laminations forming the keel had split across. The situation was extremely serious; for a boat to break her back usually spelled the end of her life. Our only hope was to make some kind of temporary repair which would enable us to sail on to Bombay. With any luck, we might be able to use the facilities of a shipyard there, and strengthen her sufficiently for us to continue on the voyage in comparative safety. We cleaned out the bilge and jammed in yards of caulking cotton and putty. Then I shaped up a wooden knee, a solid teak bracket that would stiffen the centreboard casing, and screwed it into position to try to hold the keel together. By mid-afternoon we had finished the work, and were starting to prepare for sea again, when a young Indian arrived, to announce that the mayor of Port Okha would like to meet us at 4 pm. 'Please make sure you are ready. A car will come and fetch you.'

We cleaned ourselves up as best we could and put on our best clothes. The car arrived at five to four, and we were driven down a long dirt road to the town hall. A flight of steps led into a large whitewashed room, with a long bare wooden table down the centre, and a few chairs scattered around. The mayor was a short stocky man, sporting a large handlebar moustache and dressed in traditional clothes. As we sat down on either side of him at the head of the table, we wondered uneasily what we were in for.

Half a dozen officials trooped in and sat around the table. Fortunately the one on my left was able to speak English. Glasses of iced lemonade were brought in and handed around. We sat in silence, sipping our lemonade, smiling self-consciously. After about five minutes, two dozen rather dirty and bedraggled Indians filed in and sat down on the benches to one side. Immediately the man on my left began to ask questions. Where had we come from? Were we ever afraid? How many storms had we met?

I answered them all in sequence. The mayor just looked on with a smile, understanding nothing of what I was saying—my neighbour never bothered to translate. Then a photographer arrived and took pictures of us sitting around the table. Before each photo, the mayor carefully twirled his moustache upwards and outwards with the back of his hand, and posed with arms folded, a serious, authoritative look on his face. The representatives of the working classes chatted amongst themselves, obviously at a loss to understand why they were there. I sympathised. After half an hour we all trooped outside and stood on the steps posing for yet more photographs. The car returned, we said thank you, goodbye.

I have never fathomed the significance of this meeting, but I presume that they were trying to make us welcome in the way they had seen the British acting thirty years before.

Soon after we arrived back, my English-speaking neighbour at the town hall arrived with an invitation for us to dine at his home, which we gladly accepted. We were a bit worried about leaving Nell. She hadn't eaten for four days, as she had been suffering from some kind of seasickness. In fact she was only just showing signs of recovering from her rough passage from Karachi. To tempt her appetite, we pulled in a number of small, four-inch long silvery fish. To our delight she pounced on them and devoured them whole while they were still alive. So we pulled in a few more, and more, and more. The total weight of fish she eventually ate, for a kitten of only five weeks old, was equivalent to one of us eating a 100-pound tuna at one sitting. Her small stomach stretched to bursting point; licking her lips, she waddled off into the forepeak and lay down for a long, long sleep. We stopped worrying about our Nell.

Our friend arrived punctually at 7.30, and drove us to his home, a large western-style bungalow surrounded by a high brick wall and with a small courtyard leading down from the front porch. We walked into what seemed to be the main living-room, which was sparsely furnished with a few bamboo chairs, and a small Kashmiri wood coffee-table in the centre. A single low-powered light bulb illuminated the room with a dull glow. He introduced us to his wife who namasted, bowing solemnly. We followed suit. His four daughters came in turn to bow respectfully before us.

'We are Jains,' our host said, extending his arms towards the dining-room, 'I hope you will like our vegetarian food.'

'I'm sure we shall,' I murmured politely. I caught Dave's eye-he was evidently as depressed by this news as I was. The prospect of a vegetarian meal was a blow—we were both very hungry.

The dining-room was also very bare, with walls and floor covered in large red tiles. I noticed a wash basin in the far corner, and that on the back of each of our chairs lay a small hand towel; with a chatter of noise and high-pitched giggles coming from the kitchen, I walked over and washed my hands thoroughly. I then sat down at the table regarding what lay ahead with some pessimism.

Our host bowed, said a short prayer, and called to the kitchen. The eldest daughter came in with three large stainless steel platters and laid them before us. She was a beautiful young girl of about eighteen, with delicate features, a strong chin and large shining brown eyes. She flashed a broad smile at us, so that her pearly white teeth gleamed in the dull light of the room. I winked at Dave, who was also finding it difficult to concentrate as her father described all the vegetables we were about to consume.

When the three younger daughters had filed in with dishes of steaming hot food, the eldest returned with a large bowl containing a white milky substance. She placed this gently in the centre. 'That,' he began to explain, 'is the real curry. I warn you it is extremely hot. But do try a little…'

The food surpassed all our expectations, and we finished every morsel that was put before us. The platters, about two feet in diameter, were continually re-filled by our host. At one point, I even tried a little of the curry—my blood seemed to boil, my face turned a bright red and beads of sweat streamed down my forehead. The banquet lasted for two hours. Eventually we raised ourselves with considerable difficulty, bloated with food.

When we climbed down the steps to *Hermes*, we found Nell fast asleep up forward, with a contented smile still on her face. We were up again soon after sunrise, and wandered into town, heading for the market. We bought up a quantity of potatoes, ducks' eggs and a large bunch of bananas. On our way back we called in at the naval headquarters to bid our farewells and helped them to finish their third and last bottle of whisky.

Back on board we stowed the gear ready for sea, and I went off along the beach to fill Nell's dirt box with some fresh clean sand. The two days in port had helped her to settle down to the life on board. We had caught a few more fish which would last her for a couple of days and she was becoming used to drinking a solution of dried milk powder and water. In fact the lady was already putting on weight. By mid-day we were ready to leave, and Dave climbed up forward to hoist the sails. The genoa slowly filled and the bows pulled away from the jetty; *Hermes* gathered speed and we slipped quietly out of the harbour towards the rocky breakwater. The wind had moderated but was still blowing from the north, which would help us on our way to Bombay.

As darkness fell, Nell was sitting in the stern watching the waves pass under us, when one broke and tumbled alongside. Her ears pricked up in surprise and she ran back into the forepeak. At night she would come alive, but during the heat of the day she spent most of her time lying as low as possible in the bilge, fast asleep. I was afraid that in her antics during the night she would fall overboard, so I made her a life line and tied it around her waist and shoulders.

We had already become very attached to Nell and neither of us wanted to lose her overboard.

By now Dave and I had been living together in these drastically cramped conditions for seven months. Naturally enough we discussed women. But by this stage even women had begun to pall as a topic of conversation. Politics and religion were rarely discussed; Dave was a total agnostic and since we were so far from home, the political stability of Britain did not seem to concern us.

It was now late November; although neither of us were overtly sentimental about such things, both of us were beginning to think of Christmas and of home. Where we would be for this Christmas neither of us knew; it could be on some desolate beach or out at sea fighting a gale. Wherever it was, there would be no roast turkey and Christmas pudding for us this year, no sitting around a log fire with our families and friends talking about nothing in particular, no long walks in the afternoon, breathing the crisp cold air.

But at least we had a breeze, a moderate north-westerly that was taking us down the Gujerat coast towards the Gulf of Cambay. Bombay was only 150 miles to the south-east across the mouth of the Gulf.

It took us two days to cross this shallow Gulf. Navigation was difficult, not only on account of the shoals, but also because of the small groups of fishing boats, with their nets strewn over miles of sea. Lights were only used as a last resort; at night we had to keep a careful watch for a glowing string in the water, the only indication that a fishing boat was around. On one occasion I saw some black shadows ahead. I started the outboard, switched on our masthead light and steamed towards them. Suddenly all hell broke loose—I had caught them all while they were having a quick nap. Excited yelling and shouting came from all directions, oil lamps were lit and for what seemed miles around, lanterns of all sizes were hoisted frantically into the rigging. I motored on through and came out at the end of the fleet feeling rather saucy. But at least it had brightened up an otherwise dull night watch.

The wind died just before dawn on 22 November, just as we were glimpsing the lights of Bombay off the port bow. Our naval friends in Port Okha had advised me to call Bombay on the RT before arrival, to prevent another two-hour search by customs and police. As we motored through the hot, sultry dawn mist, I switched on the transmitter and flicked the dial to 2182 KHz, the International frequency. 'Bombay Radio, Bombay Radio, this is British yacht *Hermes*, call sign Mike—November—Echo—November, calling Bombay Radio, listening out on 2182, how do you read please. Over.'

The receiver crackled and spat for a while, and then a Peter Sellers-type Indian voice came through. 'Who is that calling Bombay Radio?'

I repeated my message and sat back. 'British ship *Humees*, O.K. I read you—there are no messages for you, *Humees*. Over.'

' *Hermes* to Bombay,' I said, trying to keep a straight face. 'I would be very surprised if there were, Bombay—I wish to report my ETA to the customs for clearance please. Over.'

Consternation in Bombay. 'Hullo, Humees—I do not think there is any room in the port for you—how many tons are you. Over.'

This was too much for Dave. 'Tell him we're that bloody great British aircraft carrier,' he said over my shoulder. I explained calmly that we were one half of one ton, that we were a British yacht, a sailing boat from England. There was a long silence from the other end at this. Then the receiver crackled into life once more, asking how long we were. To which I replied that we were one-eight feet. 'Hullo, *Humees*, would you anchor one mile south-east of the main jetty—over.'

A mile away. That was too much. 'Hullo, Bombay, this is *Hermes*, we are only a small boat—a very small boat—a rowing boat—please can we come straight to the jetty. We will not take up much room. If we anchor a mile offshore no one will see us. Over.'

'I do not know if that is allowed, *Humees*. Over.'

' *Hermes* to Bombay—just inform the customs that we will contact them on arrival. Thank you, Bombay. Over and out.' I switched off before they could reply and headed into the harbour.

A cluster of small Bermudan-rigged sailing boats were moored a hundred yards off the Gateway of India; we motored in towards them and picked up a vacant mooring buoy. A number of Europeans were coming down a short slipway; the small tender dinghies, with a ragged Indian in each, scuttled around ready to take their masters out to their boats. As one group came past, a voiced hailed us. 'Aren't you the two from England ?'

'That's right,' we said simultaneously.

'Sorry. We're off sailing now for the afternoon, but please use the club. See you when we return.'

'Thanks very much,' I replied. A few minutes later one of the dinghies came alongside, to take us ashore. Nell would have to stay on board for the time being.

On shore we were directed towards the pillars of a large and elegant four-storeyed building. We were still dressed in our dirty shorts and ancient, tattered shirts; clutching our small blue sail-bags, with our not-so-clean clothes, we strolled up the short drive. The young Indian boy on duty, dressed in his smart sailor's uniform, looked somewhat surprised as two half-shaven and very dirty English sahibs walked straight into the large entrance hall and into the shower rooms.

Two very clean, carbolic-smelling sailors emerged half an hour later, dressed in rather crumpled slacks and walked into the lounge. We sat down in two comfortable wicker arm chairs and looked out over the gardens and into the streets below. Drinking our tea and eating some dainty cakes, we could easily have passed for two pukka sahibs. Outside, on the far pavement, sat a seller of crushed sugar-cane juice; alongside him, with a crude form of stove and a large boiling pot, was another native, dressed in a dirty sarong, selling a rather dubious curry by the bowl. To our right there was a large wooden hut, alongside the public toilets, and lined up outside it were dozens of youths waiting for an army medical inspection.

No shortage of recruits in India—the guarantee of food and a bed make this a much better proposition than living in the streets.

When the sailing party returned, a mass of servants rushed around the lawn erecting tables and chairs so that their masters could sit out in the cool of the evening, and drink their pink gins. When we went out to join them, we were asked the usual questions. 'What do you do in a bad storm?' 'How on earth can you live on such a small boat?' 'Are you ever frightened?' I replied to them all with the usual answers. 'Sleep.' 'We manage,' and 'Sometimes.'

Thanks to the combined efforts of a British couple and a young German diplomat, we were soon installed in a room at the Royal Bombay Yacht Club. Having cleared the necessary customs formalities, we were free to turn our attention to finding a place that could repair *Hermes*. Here the officials of the Mazagon Dock came to our assistance and generously offered to hoist *Hermes* out by crane, repair the keel and anything else that needed attention, completely free of charge.

I was now spending nearly all my time poring over charts, pilot guides and weather maps for the next half of the voyage, which posed some particularly difficult problems. It was essential that we should have the northerly monsoon to help us through the 4000 miles of the Indonesian Archipelago. This would take three months, even with the monsoon behind us. But I calculated that it would take us at least two months to sail down the Indian coast and across the Bay of Bengal to Malaysia. The monsoon only lasted five months, and had already started a month ago.

However deviously I juggled with the figures, the fact remained that we could not hope to fit six months' sailing into five months. Everything pointed to our having to stop at Singapore for nearly six months until the change of monsoon, which would undoubtedly be the end of the voyage. Finances were low, and the chance of work in Singapore for either of us was almost nil. Somehow we had to get to Singapore within the month. If we were going to reach Australia at all, we were going to have to stick our thumbs out for another ride. It would mean reducing our own sailing distance by 1000 miles, from 13,000 to 12,000. Not a drastic reduction, perhaps, but we were now asking for help from outside our own resources, and this hurt. But it would hurt even more if we had to end the voyage in Singapore. It was obvious that we must be shipped, but it took many hard hours of weighing up the pros and cons until eventually I agreed to ship her.

It was the hardest decision I had to take, I think; but once the decision had been made I felt easier in my mind. I went down to the main docks in search of any ship that might help, mainly thinking of the British India Steamship Company. It seemed to be my lucky day—one of their ships was in, and what's more it was the *Dwarka* and our old friend Captain Peter Farrel. I went on board and explained our difficulties. Pete was very sympathetic—and offered to put in a word for us with McKinnon McKenzie, their agents. Later that afternoon we formed up in front of Mr Pike, the director responsible, who told us that the *Chinkoa*, one of their ships, was due to arrive in a few weeks. 'I have to confirm this with our directors in London, but I think we can take your boat free of charge and yourselves at a nominal cost of 30 shillings per day. How does that suit you?'

'Magnificent,' I said, bubbling with happiness and relief. 'That will give us time to sail down the Indian coast for a way.'

'Well, if that's what you want to do, the *Chinkoa* will be stopping in Cochin, why not pick her up from there?'

'Even better,' I said, 'the whole thing sounds too good to be true.'

After thanking him profusely, we left his office and went straight to the Yacht Club to pick up all our papers and passports. Then we almost ran back to 'Mick and Mack', as they are affectionately called, to deal with the formalities. The rest of the day was spent in filling in reams of forms, but by early evening everything was finished.

The following morning we went back to the offices to see how things were going. The young clerk who had been dealing with us seemed a little nervous at meeting us again. 'I'm afraid there has been some trouble,' he said, looking down at the floor.

'What's up?' I asked, thinking that this offer really had been too good to be true.

'I'm sorry but I cannot explain. The customs and police would like to see you—they will tell you all about it.'

Straight to the customs building. 'I've just been told by McKinnon McKenzie that you want to see us,' I announced, not feeling in the best of moods.

'Mr Pyle and Mr Derrick?'

'Right.'

'Wait in that room, please.' He looked a little apprehensive at being confronted by two fairly large and angry Englishmen. We walked into a small cubicle, about eight feet square, with two wooden chairs and a small rough wooden table in its centre, and sat down to await developments.

For three hours we sat and waited. Eventually I stormed out. 'What the hell's going on?' I fumed at the little man behind his desk, who cringed in his chair with a look of terror on his face.

'I'm sorry,' he said meekly, 'but my superior is at the docks and I can tell you nothing until he returns.'

'Right, let's go down to the docks and see him.'

'Yes—yes, of course, follow me.'

I knew the way to the docks, and strode down the road with the customs official following at a steady trot behind. We arrived to find them checking luggage; a number of people had recently arrived from a South African ship. 'I will go and find him. Wait here please.' The little man ran off towards the far side of the shed. I saw a tea-trolley in the passenger waiting shed, strolled over, bought myself a cup of a light brown liquid and sat down on one of the benches.

An hour and four cups of tea later, I was still sitting on the bench. I stormed out of the waiting-room and back into the customs shed. The customs officer was talking to a policeman.

'Look here, you must know why we are being held.'

'I'm sorry, sir, but I have no authority to tell you.'

'But I have every bloody right to know!' Various Europeans looked across and began to talk in low whispers, with a lot of tut-tutting and shaking of their heads.

'Very well, but this is very much against regulations.' He pulled out a slip of paper from his top pocket and handed it to me. On the heading it read, 'Suspected of Spying and Smuggling—Two British sailors, Messrs

Pyle and Derrick, in British yacht *Hermes*, arrived Port Okha from Kara-chi, West Pakistan, on November 14th. On board radio transmitter with frequencies 2182, 2381, 2009, 2016, 2434, 2049, 2056, 2246, 2301 and 3446-5. Signed—Port Okha Naval Authorities.' So, our two young naval officers in Port Okha had suspected us of spying. So much for their friend-ship, not to mention their whisky.

For the following few days we lived in the Royal Bombay Yacht Club by night and went to the customs offices during the day. Every day we were kept waiting in the small cubicle for hours, questioned for a short time, and then kept waiting again. Of an evening we would sit in the Club's bar talking to the long-standing members about our day's experience. 'You must never lose your temper,' they would say. 'Do whatever they ask, kiss their boots if need be, but never be insulting.' But pride had always been my biggest failing. Every day my temper rose to full pitch. Every day we saw someone with a little more seniority, but no one would take the initia-tive to let us go free.

On the third afternoon we finally met one of the senior officials. 'I'd like to make one thing very clear,' I said. 'As a British taxpayer, I have helped finance a £25 million interest-free loan to India. Now you treat us like this. The whole thing makes me feel sick. We have not been spying and have no wish to become tied up with your childish quarrels with West Pakistan.'

'I am very sorry,' he said, leaning calmly back in his chair, 'but you must understand that we have to follow up every report of this nature that comes in. You are perfectly free to go.'

I had come prepared for another full-scale row. His quiet manner took the wind out of my sails. We said nothing and walked out.

In fact we walked into an expensive restaurant where a vivacious Eu-ropean girl was performing an erotic strip tease on the dance floor. She walked up to me and, almost sitting in my lap, began to fondle my hair. I held on to the table with one hand and to my soup spoon with the other. But at least she helped us to forget the last few days.

We found out that the *Chinkoa* was 10 days early and should be arriv-ing in Bombay within the week and leaving two days later. This ruled out

Crowd of Indonesians in a fishing boat off Java

Making an Indonesian courtesy flag as we approach Sumatra

Strange sprit-sail
schooner-rigged
fishing boats off Java

The author standing
alongside the bows
of a fishing boat in
the village of prosti-
tutes in Java

Cochin—we would have to be shipped from Bombay. I was frankly upset this time, by missing out on the sail down the Indian coast. I walked into a dirty-looking cafe with blood-red stains of betel juice splattered over its floor and walls; I needed time to think. *Hermes* would be ready for sea by now, and was probably in the water waiting for us. I had forgotten all about her during the past few days. We had a free week ahead, and in this time it should be possible to sail a couple of hundred miles southwards and back again, which would take us almost as far as Goa, the old Portuguese state. I didn't bother to finish my tea. I hailed a taxi instead.

We arrived just as the crane was swinging *Hermes* back into the water. A dozen Indian dockers handed the gear down to us and within an hour we were ready for sea once more. I lifted up the bottom boards to see if she was leaking at all—there wasn't a drop of water to be seen. A ten-foot steel guttering had been bolted on the length of her hog, which would stiffen the whole keel and prevent it from breaking across any further. Inside, wooden knees had been screwed along the sides of the centreboard casing to stiffen it and the whole covered with glass fibre. She was strong and sound once more. I thanked the dock officials, who had been so generous and so helpful, and we sailed down to the Yacht Club mooring to pick up Nell.

Nell had been having a grand time with so much room to run around in. Feeding her was no problem. Tea had always been brought to us first thing in the morning, along with the menu for breakfast, which always included fish. Our Indian servant was mildly surprised the first time we ordered three breakfasts, two bacon and eggs and one large pomfrit grilled in butter. He worked it out in the end. Mad dogs and Englishmen.

We sailed slowly down the coast for two quiet days until we arrived off the small village of Rajpuri, which consisted of a few small wood and brick houses and a large ancient Portuguese fort, built on a rocky reef a few hundred yards offshore. The local policeman, a scrawny, mean type, came out in his canoe with the inevitable ancient Lee Enfield slung around his shoulders. He immediately ordered me ashore with our documents. I went with him in his canoe, which leaked like a sieve, yelling back at Dave to bring *Hermes* in when he saw me wave from the beach.

Once back in his shack of an office he became quite pleasant. I soon found out why. 'I see you have a case of whisky on board,' he said with a sly grin.

'I'm sorry, but I'm afraid we have no alcohol of any kind.' His smile disappeared. In fact we had no spirits on board; all I could think that he was referring to was an old Vat 69 carton which was loaded with a collection of *Reader's Digest* Condensed Books. When I explained this, he was not convinced. He spoke in Hindi for a while to three other policemen, all dressed in tattered uniforms. They shrugged their shoulders and glared. He pulled a few rubber stamps out of a drawer and filled another page of our passports.

'You may go,' he said, handing them back to me.

'Thank you,' I replied. 'Sorry about the whisky.'

Somehow I had this feeling that we were not too welcome in these parts. When Dave brought *Hermes*, I suggested that we should go up river a bit to a quieter spot. 'I think we might be visited during the night if we stay.'

'Why's that?' he asked.

'They are damn sure we have a case of whisky on board.'

'Wish we bloody well had,' he said indignantly, as he went forward with an oar to push off from the beach.

We spent the following two days on the far side of the inlet, almost a mile from Rajpuri village, just relaxing on a sandy beach. For once we could lie back and forget our troubles of the past, sunbathing, with a wonderful feeling of being safe and alive, with our home lying a few yards offshore, gently bobbing to her anchor. Nell loved the life ashore, pouncing on the crabs which scuttled over the sands. I would occasionally go out on a rocky ledge and catch a few small fish for her. She would sit beside me wide-eyed, waiting for the next one to be landed, which she would devour in ten seconds flat.

On the second day we walked into a small village a mile down the beach and bought a few eggs, a bunch of bananas and a live chicken. Nell greeted us with an affectionate miaow when we arrived back on board, and I placed the trussed chicken beside her. For a full half-minute Nell and the chicken looked at one another. Then the chicken let out a loud squawk. Nell leaped two feet in the air, spitting and howling, then ran full tilt into the forepeak and did not emerge until she saw the chicken in a different form, very dead and lightly fried.

When we returned to Bombay, we found that the *Chinkoa* had already arrived. A large derrick swung above us and a hook with two large rope slings came slowly down towards us. Mazagan Docks had made up two large wooden spreaders especially for this occasion, to prevent the strops from crushing *Hermes*' frail sides. Slowly we were lifted clear of the water and hoisted on board.

Leaving a young midshipman in charge of Nell, we went ashore to complete our last task in Bombay before departure. This was to clear from customs 2000 feet of 16-mm colour-film stock. 'I am sorry, Mr Pill, but this will take a long time,' said the customs officer. I pointed out that this film was destined for television back in England, to show India to the British people, and that it might even help the Indian tourist industry. 'I am sorry, Mr Pill,' he repeated, 'but these things take time.'

'Well, to hell with you and all your bloody paper,' I stormed. 'Forget the whole thing, take it to the *Chinkoa* under bond. We've filmed every other country including West Pakistan. So far as India is concerned, that's our lot. Finish.'

'But please, Mr Pill, you must film India,' he implored.

'Sorry, but my name's Pyle. Good day.'

11

We slipped out of Bombay early in the morning of 14 December, bound for Cochin.

Once we were clear of the crowded harbour, Bobby Coates, the skipper, invited us to his cabin for a drink. Nell followed us in and was beginning to explore the bookshelves and under his bunk, when suddenly her eye rested on a budgerigar cheerfully twittering in its cage. 'Don't worry, Bobby,' I said, 'she's not interested in birds.' Nell immediately leapt up onto the table, claws extended, and tried to reach through the cage at the fluttering, squawking bird. 'Sorry about that,' I said, grabbing her by the scruff of the neck and pushing her out of the cabin door.

'Better confine that cat to her quarters. I bought that bloody bird for my daughters, who will be coming on board at Penang. I want the bloody thing flying, not stuffed.'

After a day's stop in Cochin, the MV *Chinkoa* steamed her way across the Bay of Bengal. For the few days it took us to arrive at Penang the weather was foul. Strong headwinds and squally showers swept continuously down onto our ship. 'We'd have had a hell of a job to sail across the Bay in this,' I said to Dave, as we leaned over the ship's side. 'This crossing alone would have taken us months.' In fact I slept very soundly indeed on board the *Chinkoa*, confident that we were doing the right thing. We had a large cabin each, with a separate toilet and bathroom. All mod cons for a comfortable existence. Curiously enough, we both tended to accumulate our gear around the bed and live exclusively in that small area. Having lived for so long in the confined space of *Hermes'* cockpit had affected our normal living habits in any number of ways. I had already noticed that whenever I went ashore, a large room had the effect of giving me a lonely, cold and unhomely feeling.

Hermes contained everything that we required for our simple way of life. We clung to her when in a strongly inhospitable area; she became like a child's favourite doll or teddy bear, held close to the body when alone at night. Most people were surprised to see us living happily in such cramped conditions; but to us the voyage had become a way of life, indeed our only way of life. We had now spent eight months and travelled over 9000 miles, through thirteen different countries, on what seemed now to be a perpetual search for what lay round the corner, striving desperately each day to get a little nearer Australia.

The mangrove swamps slipped by either side of the *Chinkoa*, as we slowly steamed into Port Swettenham on the Malay coast, 300 miles north-west of Singapore. Within half an hour *Hermes* had been hoisted over the side and into the muddy waters of the harbour. It was Christmas Eve; the weather was hot, muggy, very humid and oppressive—the crisp, frosty weather, the blazing log fires, the roast turkey and Christmas pudding all seemed very far away. Back to sleeping on air beds on the bottom boards of *Hermes*. Back to dehydrated food.

Having stowed all our gear, ready for the voyage through the Malacca Straits and down to Singapore, we went back to thank everyone concerned for bringing us across. Bobby's wife and two daughters had come on board and he invited us into his cabin for a farewell drink. 'Before you go,' he said, 'I've got something for you, to help you celebrate Christmas.' He rang the bell on his cabin wall. 'Ask the purser to come up, please.' The steward vanished, and the purser soon materialised holding a small hamper, which Bobby handed over to me. Its contents were covered with a white tea towel, and I lifted up one corner and peered in. The rich smells of roast duck and brandy-flavoured Christmas cake wafted up to my nostrils.

'But this is too kind...' I murmured, my mouth drooling.

'That should take care of the food. Now for the liquid.' He walked over to his cocktail cabinet and pulled out three bottles. 'Whisky, rum, gin. Should do the trick?' He handed the bottles over to Dave, whose eyes were now sparkling at the thought of Christmas Day.

Clutching our precious cargo, and with Nell already clawing at the hamper of food, we parted company with our generous friends on board the *Chinkoa* and motored out of the harbour towards the Malacca Straits.

The north-east monsoon was in full swing, and I was frankly worried about our chances of being hit by a Sumatra. These are fierce miniature cyclones, which form down the Malacca Straits with no previous warning, and build up into huge, towering cumulus, thundery clouds, with the wind at their base screaming at over sixty knots. The Admiralty pilot guide warned us that they normally form during the night with the cooling of the land masses in the mountains of Sumatra, and the colder air travels down the mountain slopes and meets with the warmer sea air; the combination is devastating.

I was hoping to reach Port Dickson by Christmas Day, so that we could beach *Hermes* by the European Yacht Club a mile south of the town. By late afternoon, we still had forty miles to go, as we droned our way past thick mangrove swamps. As the evening drew in, heavy dark cumulus clouds formed to seaward. With darkness these cloud formations began to erupt with a display of lightning that lit up the whole of the horizon. I pulled out the chart of the Malaysian coast, switched on the flashlight and began to search for some small river or creek that might give us shelter, in case one of these horrifying storms descended. The whole coast was crudely charted, and gave no indication of any shelter except Port Dickson, still twenty miles south.

We motored on, keeping a cautious eye to seaward, watching the progress of these miniature storms. As we rounded the low swampy headland, just distinguishable during the flashing of the lightning, we saw the lights of Port Dickson ahead. The storm now seemed to be surrounding us, both at sea and on the mountains inland, so that we had no escape. Suddenly I saw a string of lights in the water, stretching right across our bows. I pushed the helm hard over, while Dave, suddenly awoken by my blaspheming, came up to see what was going on. The lights were the corks of some fishing nets, bobbing in the fluorescent water, I followed this string of glowing corks for over half a mile, until I noticed the outline of a small boat ahead, silhouetted by the lightning. As I flashed the torch into her cockpit, a rather frightened face with slanting eyes peered over the gunwale, blinking in the glare of the torch. Since the Malacca Straits are overrun with Indonesian pirates from Sumatra, the poor fellow must have thought that his last hour had come. I could think of no Malaysian words, so I shone the torch onto *Hermes* and myself, to try and show that we were friendly, and then motored past him towards Port Dickson.

After dropping anchor, Dave came back into the cockpit. 'A very Happy Christmas,' I said, handing him a tumblerful of whisky.

'And to you too,' he replied, taking the tumbler and gulping the fiery liquid down in one swift movement.

I followed suit and we refilled our glasses.

'Absent friends?'

'Absent friends.'

The familiar chink of glasses floated over the harbour.

The Sumatra spared us that night. But once we reached the entrance to the port of Malacca, we were confronted with a new hazard: fish traps. Sixty-foot poles of thick bamboo, driven into the sea bed, support a platform, fifteen to twenty feet above the sea's surface, where the fisherman builds his hut and lives and works. But leading out to sea from this platform are two rows of lethal bamboo stakes, planted close together forming a funnel for the fish to swim into. Under the platform lies the net to scoop up the fish as they pass through the neck of the funnel.

These strange, fragile-looking structures creaked and groaned as the current flowed around their thin legs. As the sun began to set, they became more difficult to see. Some of them had collapsed, probably due to the fierce winds of a Sumatra, and many of the sharp ends of the stakes were just below the surface. For a boat as small and as fragile as *Hermes*, these became a real menace. If we hit one in the dark it would easily pierce our thin plywood hull. Since the Admiralty pilot guide indicated that they are found along the whole Malaysian coast, and up to ten miles offshore, I decided that from now on we would anchor every night, until we arrived at Singapore.

Our troubles were escalating. While we were negotiating the numerous reefs and islands that are dotted around the entrance to the bay of Malacca, a huge thunderstorm began to develop a few miles out to sea. A small cotton wool cumulus cloud suddenly began to grow and within half an hour had sprouted upwards and outwards until its top had become a huge anvil. For a few minutes it stayed motionless. Then, as though a sudden clap of thunder was its starting pistol, it began to move towards us. The dark shadow of rain began to descend from its bladder. Streaks of forked lightning flashed within its belly and around its side, as the huge monster slowly gathered speed towards us.

For a full half hour both Dave and I had been staring at this awe-inspiring sight. As it descended upon us, we suddenly came back to reality. 'Quick,' I shouted, 'get the main down and stick up the working jib.' The short, fat, stocky, half-naked Dave, normally incapable of speed, leapt up onto the fore deck and began to unravel all the halyards in double-quick time. I rummaged forward, found the working jib and handed it to him, keeping a wary eye upon this black mass descending even faster upon us. I just had time to trim sail, and to clip Nell to her life line, when the first fierce, terrifying squall hit. *Hermes* heeled over until her side decks were awash and water was lapping into the cockpit. I immediately grabbed the jib sheet, released it from the jamming cleat and let the sail fly. *Hermes* came up onto a more even keel and I looked ahead hoping that we were not heading into any reef, island or fish trap. Soon after the squall of wind had hit us, the rain began to fall in a cascading deluge. Dave dived under the canopy and zipped himself in, to protect both himself and our equipment below.

I had never seen rain come down with such colossal force. As I hung on grimly to the helm, my eyes stung, my nose became clogged and I had to bend my head to shelter my mouth so that I could breathe. With visibility nil and the compass out of sight below the canvas awning, I had to steer by sense and feel of the wind. As *Hermes* ploughed on towards the unknown I began to fear even more for our safety, so I put the helm around, sheeted in tightly on the mizzen and backed the jib. We would stay hove to until the storm was over. For an hour and a half, the rain just fell in a solid driving sheet of water, flattening the sea's surface, even though the wind screamed in from all directions at well over gale force. Then, quite suddenly, silence. Everything stopped. The air was still and damp, as the storm cloud had passed over us, driving in towards the shore and the mountains inland. As we sailed on southwards, Nell came out from under the awning, obviously to use her earth box. She looked inside at the brimming brown liquid, twitched her nose and wandered off towards the stern. For a while she looked around her at the water swilling around the after deck, lapping at her paws. Obviously, with so much water around, another little drop would make little difference, so she squatted on the far corner of the after deck.

As darkness began to descend, we motored up a small creek and dropped the anchor in two fathoms of water. I shall always remember that evening as one of the most beautiful, peaceful and fascinating. As we sat under the mosquito netting, with the small oil lantern casting a ghostly glow over our faces, I held a mug of hot coffee laced with rum and listened to the strange noises of the jungle shattering the stillness of the night. The fragrant smoke from the slow-burning anti-mosquito coil mingled with the smoke from my cigarette and was whisked away by the cool evening breeze. The coarse throaty croak of the bullfrog sounded all around, occasionally interrupted by the terrified scream of some small creature within the heart of the jungle. We were alone and completely at peace with the world. To have come through so much in the last eight months and survived was a wonderful feeling; one of triumph and extreme satisfaction which was very real to us just then. I settled down into my sleeping bag, the rum sending a soothing warmth through my body, and slept that night as soundly as if I hadn't a worry in the world.

By the following evening we managed to reach a small village on the extreme south-western tip of Malaysia. I noticed a mass of fish traps ahead so we anchored for the night, close to the village, expecting to make Singapore by noon of the following day. At first light I was awoken by *Hermes* being tossed to and fro by a short steep sea. I peered out from under the canopy, and to my amazement I saw that the nearest land was no longer 100 yards, but over two miles away. During the night *Hermes* had dragged her anchor and had gaily sailed through the mass of fish traps on her own. 'We might as well pack it in,' I said to Dave, who was blearily looking around in disbelief. 'It looks as though she can sail herself to Australia.'

The shipping began to get thicker, all heading towards the thriving international port. We sailed through the narrow entrance of Keppel Harbour, past all the large ocean-going ships, and continued around the headland to the thriving small boat harbour fronting the main city of Singapore, which is about the most congested harbour in the world. Small coastal cargo ships, Chinese junks, tugs and wooden barges were moored at random within the breakwater. Small tugs, towing strings of six or more barges, weaved their way like Chinese paper dragons through this conglomeration. With all the traffic, the water inside was rougher than in the open sea. I had wanted to clear customs here, but decided that it was too dangerous to leave *Hermes* along the harbour wall; I carefully manoeuvred her out past the breakwater again and headed north-eastwards towards Changi, which we reached just before midnight.

Only one country now lay between us and Australia, the long string of South Sea islands of the Indonesian archipelago.

Naturally, I was anxious that *Hermes* should be as seaworthy as possible. I wanted to check her over for any leaks and cracks that might have been caused by hauling her in and out of the water by the *Chinkoa*'s derricks, and especially for teredo worm, a type of thin marine tapeworm that can burrow into the wood and hollow out whole planks, leaving only a thin shell to break up in the first minutes of any bad weather. None of her rigging had been changed since leaving England, and I wanted to make sure that this was still strong enough to cope with the strong winds associated with the north-east monsoon. So the following morning we got in touch with the officers of the RAF sailing club, who came down to help us slip *Hermes*, and put her in a position where we could carry out any necessary repairs.

By the evening all our gear and equipment had been stowed in a small shed belonging to the yacht club. I phoned two old friends of mine, Dave and Christobel Milner, who immediately drove over with a pressing invitation for all three of us to stay with them while we were in Singapore.

It was now 31 December, New Year's Eve, and we had no plans of how we would celebrate this annual event. Singapore is one of the most corrupt and decadent cities in the world. 'Just find a bar, and take it from there,' they suggested.

We did just that; we found a bar. I can remember a few isolated incidents, such as my collapsing onto a bar table which shattered beneath me, and yelling at some large voluptuous negro singer, 'Take 'em off, take 'em off.' For eight, glorious, wild and hazy hours, we forgot the trials and tribulations of the past eight months.

For over two weeks we stayed with the Milners, working almost full-time on *Hermes*. She was stripped right down; every nut, bolt, screw and nail was carefully examined. Any joint that seemed to be opening was reinforced, the rigging was checked over and any badly worn shackles and cordage replaced. Meantime Nell enjoyed herself ashore in the flat. I had hoped at one time that we could have left her with Dave and Christobel; but she found that peeing in the large pots containing rubber-tree plants was more fun than using her dirt box. The rubber-tree plants slowly turned yellow and withered away. She then discovered she could leap the six feet from the dining-room table into a large tropical fish tank. Slowly Dave and Christobel's collection of fish disappeared, and Nell became fatter. Nell was not invited to stay behind.

On 15 January I went along to the Royal Air Force meteorological offices to check on the weather situation. I was warned against setting off while the north-east monsoon was blowing. 'The winds can be very strong and the isolated storms very fierce and frequent,' said the met officer.

'But we have to use these following winds, if we are to make Australia this year.'

'Well—' he said hesitantly, 'if you think your boat…'

'My boat can outride these winds,' I said confidently.

I left the met office deep in thought. Perhaps I was being rather foolhardy in leaving now, but it was a calculated risk. To have the headwinds of the south-west monsoon would not affect us for the first 500 miles as we would be sheltered by the island of Sumatra, but once we were south of the Equator, they become south-easterly and are very strong across the Timor Sea. *Hermes* was too small to sail against a strong monsoon wind, yet I was certain that it was right to sail now.

Early in the morning of 17 January we left Changi, on a southwesterly course, bound for Sumatra, Indonesia. Nell stood on her hind legs, looking over the gunwale towards the land as it slipped by, with a sorrowful expression. The wind was blowing steadily from the north-east and we set the twin genoas, which we boomed out on either side of the main mast, like the large brown wings of some strange bird.

The low-lying jungle and mangrove swamps of the south-eastern coast of Sumatra were spread out before us—an area well known for pirates, more so even than the Persian Gulf. Almost every day in Singapore we had read in the papers of some Malayan or Singapore fishing boat being raided by pirate craft from Sumatra. Little was known of their hideouts but everything indicated, from the areas of their attacks, that they came from the swampy shores of the central east coast of Sumatra, probably from some small bamboo village up the many thousands of miles of rivers that snake their way through the steaming jungle. I was sceptical, up to a point. None of the Arab dhows that we had seen sailing through the Gulf and Arabian Sea had bothered us; usually they had given us a friendly wave of greeting. On the other hand, this hardly guaranteed us a friendly reception at these jungle river villages.

We made our landfall north of the island of Kundur at the mouth of the River Kampar. The admiralty chart gave no indication of any habitation along this coast, but some RAF aerial charts did show some small brown blobs with *kampong* written alongside them. One such blob was shown in a narrow strait between the island of Kundur and Onggut, so I decided to head for this village. With our fingers crossed, and a moderate northerly wind blowing, *Hermes* creamed her way through the strait. Weird tangled roots of mangrove trees and large feathery fronds of fernlike plants slipped by on either side, as the narrow channel wound through the jungle for more than ten miles. Just as we came round the final bend, before sailing back into the Java Sea once more, a village suddenly appeared, half hidden by the jungle. We peered ahead at the cluster of bamboo huts, each jutting out on its platform over the river. Two small very tanned men wearing tattered uniforms were sitting in a little wooden motor launch which was gently bobbing alongside a rickety wooden jetty. 'We'll just sail past, Dave,' I said, 'but do try and look a bit more friendly.'

I brought *Hermes* abreast of the launch. At first the two men looked in numbed disbelief at our yellow craft. I waved and put on my broadest smile. Their faces suddenly lit up, and they waved and chattered excitedly at one another. They dropped their arms suddenly as we sailed straight past. I looked behind and saw one jump on to the jetty and run towards one of the huts. 'I think we've started something,' I said to Dave, who seemed totally unconcerned as he peered glumly ahead.

We lost sight of the village as we sailed back out to sea, but within half an hour the small launch came out from the strait and motored directly for us. I tried to make out how many people were on board. 'I think one is holding a rifle. We'd better heave to and wait.' When the launch arrived, one of the men started talking rapidly, pointing back towards the village. I tried to indicate that I could not understand and produced a mass of papers which I had collected from the Indonesian Embassy in Singapore. He took them and looked with a blank expression at the script he obviously could not read. Again he spoke and pointed back to the village. I didn't like the look of that rifle, so we headed back in convoy. The launch tied up alongside the dilapidated jetty and I brought *Hermes* alongside. A crowd, fifty or more men, women and children, all dressed in gaily coloured sarongs, had gathered to watch the fun. 'You had better stay here and keep an eye on things,' I said, 'I'll go up and see what's cooking.'

The crowd parted as I followed the man through a narrow dirt street to a small timbered building. Inside was a group of young men, some sitting on a hard wooden bed, others on a few wooden chairs, the sum total of the furniture in the room. The floors were of bare earth and only a coloured picture of Suharto and a calendar helped break the monotony of the wooden plank walls. One of the men asked in sign language if I would like a drink. I nodded and smiled, and he spoke to a young girl who had been peering through the doorway.

A sudden outburst of shouting and screaming came from the direction of the jetty. Half the occupants of the room immediately dived out of the doorway shouting and laughing outside as they looked in the direction of the channel. I was too deep in my own thoughts to take much notice. The young girl returned with a glass and four large bottles of beer. All four bottles were put before me. I looked at the label—Tiger Beer from Singapore; I turned the bottle round and there was a large blue stamp—'Singapore, duty not paid.'

After I had downed two of the bottles, the official with my papers came back and indicated that I should follow. I tried to show my thanks for the beer, and left the room. As we walked up the street I noticed that many of the villagers were driving around on brand new Honda motor-bikes; sparkling new outboard motors were propped up outside some of the small wooden houses. When my companion offered me a cigarette, a Rothmans with 'Singapore, duty not paid' stamped along its side, I began to wonder. Something was wrong.

We arrived at the only brick building in the village, where two men dressed in smart western tropical suits were sitting out on a veranda, drinking coffee. One of them got up and came over to me. 'I am sorry you were stopped,' he said in perfect English. 'But you must understand that we have to check on anyone coming into Indonesia.'

'Yes, of course,' I replied, 'but everyone has been very kind.'

'Please come inside,' he said, 'I doubt if you have eaten. I will get you some food and coffee.'

I went into the sparsely furnished room. 'Well, your papers are in order,' he said, smiling, 'please sit down. Tell me—why have you come here?' I explained that we were on our way to Djakarta, and wanted to sail down the Sumatra coast to see something of the villages. 'There is only one thing that bothers me,' I said. 'We heard in Singapore about pirates operating from this area. I hope you won't mind me asking, but is this true?'

'Oh—pirates,' he said quietly, looking at me under lowered eyelids. 'Let me explain. Our people are very poor, those from Singapore are rich. Maybe sometimes we would like some of those things which the Singapore and Malay people have, so sometimes our poor fishermen go over there and get some good nets or an engine. It is just the way of life.' He shrugged his shoulders. It was a while before the truth dawned —he was telling me, in the nicest possible way, that they were just a bunch of sea robbers. A nice, friendly, hospitable bunch of robbers, of course.

I subsequently found out that my companion was a naval officer, but I decided it would not be prudent to enquire too closely about his ships. When we had finished, we set off back to the village. The road ran through a short stretch of dense jungle and I could hear a variety of birds and ani-

Timber boat, low in the water, anchored off a river ready to sail to Djakarta

Children from Reo sailing upriver with us to the village, having made sails from their sarongs

One of Tjungy's men in Reo climbing a palm tree for coconuts

Slicing coconuts for copra at Tjungy's plantation

mals in the undergrowth. 'What sort of wildlife is there to be found in Sumatra?' I asked innocently.

'We have most animals and birds of the tropics, including many tigers,' he said.

'Tigers!'

'Oh yes. We had one here two weeks ago which killed two of the villagers.' I quickened my pace.

We arrived at a small hut, a hundred yards from the waterfront, where Dave was sitting at a small table, drinking a bottle of beer. He looked as though he had seen a ghost. 'What's up, mate?' I asked.

'That bloody jetty! Soon after you left, it collapsed!' Apparently so many people were standing on it that it just crumpled up. The water around *Hermes* had suddenly become a writhing mass of bodies, with mothers crying for their children and children screaming for their mothers. Fortunately the launch was between *Hermes* and the jetty; the launch had taken the brunt of the collapse, and almost capsized. *Hermes* had escaped undamaged and fortunately no one had been hurt.

I looked up at the naval officer who had been hearing the same story from another Indonesian official. They were both rocking with laughter, finding the whole incident quite hilarious. We grinned at each other stupidly—the humour was infectious. By mid-afternoon we had bidden farewell to our first Indonesian village, and were sailing southwards once more towards Amphitrite Bay, where I was hoping to enter the delta of the Indragiri river, and so penetrate farther into the Sumatran jungle. On 19 January 1970 the log book read: CROSSED EQUATOR AT 16.50 HOURS LOCAL TIME—IN THE SOUTHERN LATITUDES AT LAST.

For a full two days we sailed southwards through the inlets of the river delta into the heart of the jungle. We passed several small bamboo hut villages, but were never challenged. Wild boar, digging under the roots of the mangrove trees, were much more startled as we passed by, crashing off through the dense undergrowth with loud grunts and snorts. Flying squirrels, less agile at moving in the thick jungle, stayed high above us, gliding from tree top to tree top in search of nuts and fruit. Groups of monkeys squealed and chattered around the water's edge; sitting on some rotten tree trunk, they watched us pass with total unconcern, while they scratched and groomed themselves.

In the evening we would stop alongside the river bank, and as darkness fell the jungle noises penetrated the layer of mist settling over the still, swampy, mosquito-infested waters. The weird, frightening, Hollywood-type jungle that we had been brought up on seemed a long way away from this strange and wonderful environment. For me the jungle spelled peace and tranquillity, spiced with an air of the unknown. What lay beyond the river bank, in that thick dark mass? What caused those strange noises at night? A tiger, some small animal being killed by a predator—all part of the cruel, fierce, primitive world of survival. We, too, were engaged in our own, self-inflicted battle for survival. As we lay down to sleep, the deadly malaria-carrying mosquitoes droned quietly, flying outside our net, trying to find a way in to feast on our blood. Only the sounds of the Sumatra jungle penetrated our small world.

We left the delta on 22 January and sailed southwards to Bangka, and Muntok, the island's capital, where we put in for fresh provisions, fuel and water. Bangka is a rocky and mountainous island, a pleasant change from the low mangrove swamps along the Malayan and Sumatran coast. It was first administered by the Dutch, and later, in the mid to late eighteenth century, was taken by the British. The head man at that time, hearing of the British arrival, organised his men to kill every Dutch inhabitant, to try and please the British. On hearing about this massacre, the British Authorities were far from pleased and he was banished from the island. Over fifty years later the island came back to Dutch hands as an exchange for Malacca on the Western Malaysian coast.

We sailed through the Bangka straits and stopped at a small sandy beach, fringed by palm trees, to wash off some of the accumulated filth and grime from our bodies. As we splashed around in the fresh, clear water, we decided that it was about time we taught Nell how to swim. So having moored a few yards offshore, we gently lowered her into the water. She squirmed and wriggled a bit at first; but once she was completely immersed, she struck out strongly for the shore. Dave was there to catch her, and the performance was repeated a few times until we were both satisfied that she could swim adequately in an emergency. I took *Hermes* farther out. We dived in and swam ashore.

Nell had now decided that water was quite pleasant after all. Standing on the stern of *Hermes*, she watched us for a minute as we wandered along the beach, gave a shrill cry and leaped in. Within half a minute she was streaking up the beach heading straight for the undergrowth. We tried to go after her, but where Nell would go neither of us could follow. I managed to find a small clearing twenty yards in through the thick vegetation, and waited for her to come out. I could hear her howling as she wandered about. Then a small white and ginger face peered out from the jungle like a miniature tiger on the prowl. I dived in and grabbed her by the scruff of her neck. 'Got you, my girl. Thank God I got you before someone else!' Nell would have made a tasty dish for a python.

We sailed on towards Tg Penet, where I had decided to leave the Sumatra coast and sail across the Java Sea to Djakarta. For the third and fourth days we had little wind and crept along the coast, using the land and sea breezes to take us out of this area of doldrums. I had hopes of finding a village along the coast where we could replenish provisions; the dehydrated food from England was almost exhausted, and we had not bought a great deal from Muntok, as food was usually cheaper in the smaller villages. When we had sailed almost 200 miles since Muntok without sighting any habitation, we came across a fishing fleet of sailing canoes, accompanied by a larger motor launch. I sailed up alongside the launch and a group of cheerful, half-bearded Javanese brigands took our mooring lines. They would have passed for the fiercest looking Javanese cut-throats who sailed upon these seas, but we were beginning to know our way around. The fact that we could both now speak a few words of Indonesian undoubtedly helped.

I climbed on board to meet the skipper, and had to pick my way carefully over a number of bodies lying fast asleep on the decks. He offered me a glass of thick black coffee, half full of coarsely ground coffee beans, which I gladly accepted before mentioning our problem. He pulled out a dirty, tattered chart and began to scan the area. A nameless river flowed out into the sea ten miles to the south. Twelve miles up this river a kampong was marked, where he said we would find food. I handed around some Rothmans; we sat down for a short chat in sign language, with a spattering of Indonesian, and I admired the engine he had on board—always the pride and joy of any motor launch owner anywhere.

We arrived at the river in mid-afternoon, and sailed through a small fleet of timber boats, moored just off the mouth. These forty-foot double-ended craft, with huge lateen sails furled around the yard, were so loaded with timber that they had no more than six inches of freeboard. Why they were moored there I had no idea—perhaps they were waiting for a fair wind to take them to Djakarta. It was early evening, however, by the time we came around the final bend in the river to see the village ahead, a couple of dozen houses in a jungle clearing of about ten acres. I brought *Hermes* alongside a small wooden jetty and stepped ashore.

I walked into the village looking for a market and found one hut which had a few vegetables and baskets of fruit outside. A crowd began to assemble: not the usual smiling crowd, but a hostile lot, scowling and chattering excitedly to one another. I turned round and walked back to *Hermes*, trying to look totally unconcerned. 'Hey, mate,' I said, 'this lot don't seem to be all that friendly.'

'Noticed that myself,' Dave replied. 'But how would you feel if a total stranger suddenly walked in and wandered through your village?' His words brought me up with a jolt. We had been voyaging for so long, wandering into different countries and different villages until it had become our natural way of life. We had ceased to think how strange these new places were, or of how people might think of us as strangers. If we wanted food, we would just stop for some where we could find it—and that was that. I was frankly out of my depth.

Eventually I decided to try and talk to them. One of them, dressed in a sarong but with a fairly clean shirt, answered my request by telling me that they had no food. I pointed to the wooden hut with the vegetables outside, but he repeated that there was no food to be had there.

'Better get the hell out of here, Dave,' I said. I jumped back on board *Hermes* and started the motor. Within a few minutes the village had disappeared around the bend and we were on our way back towards the open sea.

Nell came out from under the canopy as we motored on down the river, and started running up and down the top of the sun awning. Our main canopy had begun to wear and we found that, during the torrential downpours we met along this coast, it would leak badly. To counteract this, we rigged the white sun awning over the blue canopy. Nell would scamper along the ridge of the awning and run up the mast, slide down and run back to the cockpit. This evening she became more excited than usual, and halfway back to the cockpit she missed her footing. Her back legs slipped down one side; wide-eyed with fear, she slowly slid down the smooth white terylene, desperately trying to dig her claws in, and with a gentle splash she went over the side. I quickly leaned back to the motor and closed down the throttle, slamming the helm hard over. 'Girl overboard,' I yelled to Dave, who was brewing up some tea below. I brought the boat to a standstill and we both watched Nell swim the few yards to *Hermes* in the fastest and strongest stroke she had performed to date. I grabbed her by the scruff of her neck and hauled one very wet and bedraggled cat on board. Dave dried her down with an old cloth and she waddled off for'ard, none the worse.

The following night, with a light to moderate north-westerly blowing, I laid a course on the chart for Djakarta, 130 miles to the south-east. The night was peaceful, no thunderstorms came close to us but we could see the odd flash and eruption to the north. In the early hours of the following morning the situation changed dramatically. Low grey clouds scudded above us, obliterating the clear star-studded sky. A strong tide runs through the Sunda Strait between Sumatra and Java, and its effects were felt even fifty miles north, wind over tide making the sea exceptionally confused. As dawn broke, the scene was awe-inspiring; a large sea was running in from the north-east, the direction of the South China Sea that is continually hit by cyclones during this monsoon. But from the north-west, due to the increase of wind, another sea was building up, and with a strong north-going current the scene was utter confusion. I was amazed at the way *Hermes* rode each wave, easily lifting her stem and hardly shipping a drop of water.

I had still an hour left to do on my watch, while Dave lay below curled up in his sleeping bag, trying to get some sleep. The dawn was chilly, unusual for these parts, and I had donned a full suit of oilskins. Both the sea and the sky were grey and a fine drizzle added to the general misery. My eye was caught by something in the water just off the starboard bow. I looked again, but saw nothing but the tumbling crests of the waves. Perhaps it was just my imagination. Suddenly a tall black narrow fin broke surface. My mouth dropped open and I looked in utter disbelief and horror. A huge dark shape cruised beneath this fin, and slowly circled *Hermes*. When it broke surface and let off a loud snort my mouth went dry and I became rigid with intense fear. It was a killer whale, the most ferocious creature known within our oceans. For what seemed like hours, but could only have been seconds, I stood, watching, wondering if it would do what it had done to many others, if it would charge our small frail boat. With one sweep of its tail it would smash it to pieces, leaving Dave and myself floundering helplessly in the water. With my hand clenched tight on the helm, all I could do was pray: pray that it was only curious. I steered carefully, to avoid a collision, which might arouse it into a frenzy. Then, as quickly as it had come, it slipped away below the surface.

For a full five minutes I searched the water around us, but could see no sign of this frightening creature. Dave was still asleep, and Nell curled up in a corner. I wiped my face with the back of my hand, and found it trickling with a mixture of sweat and rain. To survive such conditions is not solely a reflection upon the craft, especially when it is open, unballasted and so vulnerable to these conditions as was *Hermes*. It doesn't necessarily take a special kind of person to withstand days, weeks and even months of scorching heat, little food and water, numerous gales and storms, and visiting whales. But when wet, cramped and cold, with the boat pitching and tossing in a bad sea, the rain lashing down in torrents, we had to accept that what was happening was due to choice, our choice. Nobody had asked us to embark on this mad voyage. But as long as we could keep our morale high, trying to laugh it off when things looked grim, we would survive. It wouldn't, it couldn't last for ever; mother nature would be kinder to us later on. To survive is to accept these conditions as inevitable, as a way of life and to make the best of them.

Early in the evening of 2 February we sighted the city and docks of Djakarta.

12

WE MARCHED UP TO THE RECEPTION DESK inside the new ultra-modern British Embassy. The receptionist glanced up, obviously wondering about the sudden strong smell. 'We've just arrived from England in a small sailing boat,' I announced. 'I don't know if anyone here has heard about us, but we were hoping to meet President Suharto.'

'You must be Mr Pyle and Mr Derrick,' she exclaimed, with evident relief. 'We've heard about you all right, from the Foreign Office in London. They also said that your father is extremely worried. You're two weeks overdue and he feared you were lost.'

My poor father. Not for the first time I felt stricken with guilt. 'Do you think we could cable him—that we're both alive and well and the boat's in good shape?'

'I'll make sure that that goes off straightaway.'

We were shown into a small office upstairs, with a complex system of charts and maps of the Far East, and other pictures of aircraft of all shapes and sizes, hung around the wall. Here we were greeted by the Air Attaché, Wing Commander Chick, a tall, distinguished-looking man, who immediately ordered a pot of tea and invited us to stay at his home for as long as we were in Djakarta.

'That's very kind of you,' I said, 'I hope we won't be putting you or your wife to too much trouble.'

'Oh, I shouldn't think so,' he replied. 'We've a spare room with two beds. You didn't have anyone else on board besides yourselves?'

'Well, we did have a cat,' I said hesitantly; 'but soon after we arrived she ran off up the jetty, with a tom cat in hot pursuit.'

'Oh, I should think she'll be O.K. They like cats here.'

Within three days we received a reply from the President's palace that he would receive us at his home on the morning of 11 February, in six days' time. I promptly took to my bed for three days, with a temperature of 103°F. It was only 'flu, but I thanked my lucky stars that I was in such good hands, and not out at sea, where without drugs a bad case could be a killer. Soon after I recovered we were both invited to an Embassy party for the younger British and European residents within Djakarta. We tried to behave politely, but could hardly help noticing that conversation seemed to revolve exclusively around two subjects: the number of parties that were going on within the European community, and what they had all done wrong to deserve such a god-awful posting. Such an attitude may be common, for all I know; we had not met it before, at least not in such a concentrated form. After three weeks of sailing past what was supposedly the worst area of Indonesia, I had developed a love for this country unsurpassed by that for any other community that I had met throughout my voyaging. We slipped away as soon as we decently could.

President Suharto lived in a bungalow along an avenue of similar bungalows, a most unassuming location in fact for a leader of over 88 million people. There were no guards, unless you count the large stuffed Sumatran tiger mounted at the entrance. He greeted us in person as we entered, smiled as we shook hands and sat us down in arm chairs close by a large fish tank in his drawing-room, full of the most vividly coloured fish that inhabit the seas around the Indonesian Archipelago.

It was all very informal. For about ten minutes the interpreter stayed, while tea and cakes were served. We had been briefed by the Wing Commander that the President could speak English, but that the interpreter would be on hand in case we asked any awkward political questions. (This would allow the President time, while the question was being translated, to think of a good answer.) But neither of us were what could be called political animals. We both had, and still have, quite strong political views, to the left of centre. We were simple sailors, however, with no inclination to lob out any loaded questions about SEATO. The interpreter finished his tea and left us to it.

We sat and chatted for about an hour on Indonesia, the beauty of the islands, the fish, the colour and abundance of seashells and the friendliness of the people. It was an unforgettable experience; it was so relaxed that at any moment, I expected a horde of laughing, smiling children to come running in. When I handed him our gift of a silk dressing gown, he seemed genuinely delighted. He got up and walked into another room, returning a few minutes later with two signed copies of his biography and a beautiful casket of Indonesian hand-beaten silver.

Our stay in Djakarta had almost come to an end. We thanked the kind Wing Commander and his wife, and the two of us moved back on board *Hermes*. Neither of us mentioned Nell, but we were both thinking of her, hoping that she had found herself a happy home and a tom. But at dawn, with perfect timing, a familiar white and ginger shape came bounding down the wooden jetty towards us. She too had had her fling ashore, and now thought it time to move on.

'Nell, old girl, where have you been?' I cried. She replied with a long, high-pitched miaow, and jumped on board, purring loudly, as she muzzled her nose against my face.

We both made a great fuss of her. Dave was beaming with delight—I had seldom seen him so moved. 'Hullo, Nell, you stupid mog,' he said in his affectionate way. After a full ten minutes of fussing and fondling, Nell went for'ard under the canopy. Dave went up on the foredeck and hoisted the sails, while I untied the warps and pulled in the fenders; slowly *Hermes*, with her full complement of crew, slipped out of Djakarta bound on the last leg towards Australia.

As we slipped outside the protecting breakwater, we hit a large sea running in before the winds of the north-west monsoon. Nell suddenly decided that she had made a mistake in coming back on board; she went for'ard and was violently sick on my sleeping bag. As the steep and thunderous beam sea smashed over *Hermes*' port side, all our equipment that we so painstakingly dried out in port became wet and sodden in seconds. When we had rounded the headland, our progress became more comfortable and *Hermes* rode the seas easily on her port quarter.

The north Javanese coastline is a total contrast to that of the east coast of Sumatra. Lush green fertile plains sweep down to the shore, from a towering range of volcanic mountains running the whole length of the island. Java was beautiful. The perfectly shaped volcanoes, rising to over 10,000

feet, showed wisps of sulphur curling away from their peaks. The sway-
ing palm trees that fringed the shoreline beckoned us to relax on the pure
white sandy beaches. It was as though a picture from some fairy-tale book
had been torn out and placed before our very eyes.

The coastline east of Djakarta consists of a series of low headlands.
The charting is poor, and navigation lights almost nonexistent. As darkness descended, I decided to sail around and behind one of the headlands
for shelter. We could see two or three oil lanterns, presumably a small village that was tucked into the sheltered corner of the bay, and I headed
towards them. We anchored about 150 yards out, and settled down for the
night.

I was just beginning to doze off when suddenly some native drums began to pound away on shore.

'Cannibals,' Dave muttered. He turned over on his other side and
began to snore. After the drummer had done his solo turn, two or three
flutes came in to accompany him. As I slipped into a deep sleep, lulled by
the sounds from the shore, my imagination was working overtime. Drums
and flutes? Must be dancing women somewhere.

Early the following morning I looked up from my breakfast to see a
dug-out canoe coming swiftly towards us, paddled by three half-naked
Indonesians and one other sitting at the bow, wearing a black shirt and
a chequered sarong. Smiling broadly, the latter indicated that he wanted
us to go ashore. I lifted up a plateful of fried eggs, and tried to show him
that we would come ashore when we had finished. We carried on eating
our breakfast. The canoe returned a few minutes later, and I saw that our
black-shirted friend was brandishing a rifle. Still smiling, he again indicated that we must go ashore. I have always believed that a rifle in irrespon-
sible hands is a very persuasive instrument; we followed him in through a
narrow river mouth to a small kampong.

From the smell we could tell that the covered yard in the centre of the
village was the fishmarket. Our black-shirted friend, probably some police
or customs official, took us towards one of the two dozen or so bamboo
huts around the yard. The interior was furnished with a couple of battered wooden chairs and a string bed in the far corner. When our friend

showed no interest in our papers and passports, we deduced that he had only called us in out of curiosity, to find out who we were and where we were going. I asked him about the drums and flutes that we had heard during the night; he got up and imitated women dancing. Ah, I thought so.

We wandered around looking at the strange fishing craft pulled up on the beach, resembling canoes of the North American Indians, and watching the fishermen mending nets and making large anchors out of thick bamboo. To our surprise, a group of young women came down to the water's edge, took off their sarongs and began to bathe in the narrow creek. When we had recovered from the shock—some were astonishingly beautiful—we dragged our eyes away and walked up to the other end of the village. There we found another group of women, sitting around in a circle, fingering each other's hair, picking out the lice, popping them into their mouths and crushing them with their teeth. The ardour was quelled.

As darkness fell, village activity slowed down as most people went home. But by ten o'clock it erupted into life once more. Lanterns were lit on top of tall bamboo poles in the centre. A man brought out a fishbox, placed it below a central pole, sat down, took out a notebook and began to write down a list of names along one side of the page. The band emerged from one of the huts and seated themselves a few yards away. Then came the dancing girls, about two dozen young girls, twelve- to fifteen-year-olds, all dressed up in their western-style mini-skirts. The drums began to beat, and the flutes to blow a shrill toneless whistle. The girls began to dance around the lanterns, slowly at first, gradually speeding up to a frenzy. A crowd had gathered around, mainly young fishermen and youths we had watched at their work earlier in the day.

One of the youths walked up to one of the girls, slapped her heartily on the shoulder and walked off into the darkness, followed at a distance of a few yards by the girl. This seemed to be the sign for action. Other youths came out from the crowd, selected their girls and walked off to different parts of the village, while Dave and I stood watching, our mouths open in astonishment. Within a few minutes the first girl came back, walked up to the man sitting below the pole and handed over a note. He slipped the money into the box, and ticked her name on his list. For a full hour we watched, keeping our eye on one girl in particular; within the hour she went with a total of seven different men. Some of the young men whom we had talked to earlier tried to encourage us to join in the fun. Somehow we felt that such a rapid turnover was not our scene.

At midnight the girls were still dancing, the drums and flutes were still playing, and we left them to it. One of the girls had served our supper at the police friend's house. Our host had explained, while we sat on his floor, eating his rice and boiled fish, that this troupe travelled from village to village, spending a month or so in each one. I had little idea, at the time, of their other function.

We left the creek at first light, but by mid-day had been forced to reduce sail to the working jib. Large dark threatening clouds had begun to roll in from the north-east; soon the winds were upon us, strong and squally and fierce, with rain lashing down, reducing visibility to a few yards. *Hermes* surfed on like an unbroken stallion straining at the reins. I altered course farther to seaward, to give us a wide clearance of a headland five miles in front. The localised storm passed overhead after giving us an hour of living hell, but was followed at half-hourly intervals by other similar fierce, and frightening squalls.

During one of the lulls I saw the low-lying marshy headland which protected the Bay of Tjirebon. Five miles south of the headland lay Tjirebon bank, a vast expanse of mud and sand jutting ten miles out to sea, and charted as having only six to eight feet of water covering it at low tide. It was now half tide, so I estimated a maximum covered of ten feet. To skirt the bank meant a detour of twenty miles, and we were both looking forward to finding shelter. I decided, after consulting the chart very carefully, to cross the bank two miles offshore, where there was some indication of a slightly deeper channel; since this was not marked by any buoys or withys, very careful and precise navigation would be required to find it.

I could soon see the tumbling crests ahead, as the monsoon swell hit the shallower water. I took a series of bearings on the land and lined *Hermes* up for where I estimated the channel to be. With fingers crossed I headed directly towards the bank of short steep swell, its crests breaking, of six to eight feet in height. If I had misjudged our entrance, she would hit her bottom in their troughs and smash her hull to pieces. Close on the starboard bow I saw two poles jutting out at a rakish angle, and then the line of a half-submerged copra boat. It was a grim warning. I was still taking continuous sights on the land, marking our position on the chart, as we slowly sailed on. Then the short steep seas gave way to a long easy swell. We were over the bank and could breathe freely once more. When we reached a quiet stretch of water at the mouth of a small creek, we anchored and settled down to cook a meal, thankful that the day was over.

The farther we sailed along the north Javanese coast, the more the monsoonal winds began to weaken.

We still had over 1500 miles to sail before reaching Darwin, and I was afraid that the south-east monsoon, which would give us a dreaded head-on wind, would begin before we could cross the storm-infested Timor and Arafura Seas. Our outboard was still working, but the farther we travelled eastwards, into the less inhabited islands of the Indonesian Archipelago, the more difficult it became to buy fuel. Yet for all these things, I still did not want to hurry through these lovely islands. I wanted to stop and see the people and live with them. Dave took the opposite view. He was talking now more and more of Australia and of what he would do when we arrived. To a degree, the essence of the voyage for him was beginning to change.

As we sailed on for 400 miles towards the island of Bali, the days were not hot, clear and sunny. Sailing after mid-day became extremely oppressive, with high humidity and temperature. To amuse myself, I tried as many variations as humanly possible with our limited food. Our diet became rice with some dried soup poured over the top, or flapjacks made from just flour and water and, if we were lucky, a mixture of potato powder, mango chutney and Marmite formed into a cake and fried in margarine. We also tried different concoctions of curry, and bubble and squeak from the dried vegetables. None were very successful.

Sanitary arrangements aboard *Hermes* posed no problem as long as the weather stayed quiet and calm. A three-foot length of knotted terylene was fixed permanently onto the mizzen mast: By hanging on grimly to this line and placing one's backside over the stern, we had an admirable self-flushing toilet laid on; if a large sea was running up astern, it did more than flush.

On 28 February we sailed into the small harbour of Singaradja, on the northern coast of the island of Bali. With *Hermes* safely tucked up a small sheltered creek close by the town, Dave and I jumped on board a rusty pre-war bus and travelled through the mountains southwards to the town of Dan Pasar. It was swarming with tourists, from Europe, Australia and America, both the very rich variety and long-haired hippies. For the rich, Bali represents the palm-swaying tropical South Sea island, with half-naked beautiful women; to the hippy brigade, an easy-going and inexpensive life. It was all so false, so unlike the true Indonesia we had seen to date. Within twenty-four hours we were back on the bus.

We set off eastwards in fine weather towards the less fashionable islands. As we rounded the northern-most headland a small cumulus cloud slowly drifted in towards us and increased in size as we watched. We quickly reduced sail to a working jib again, only just in time before the first squall hit us. Within minutes I realised that we were heading for trouble in a big way, that this storm was probably going to be worse than any of the others we had experienced. From almost flat calm, a long, steep, heavy swell began to run in from seaward. But the torrential downpour of rain had no calming effect upon the sea and we began to find the going extremely dangerous. The waves were unusual, and *Hermes* couldn't ride them. We soon began to ship gallons of water. With the lee shore only half a mile to starboard the situation looked serious. The outboard had little effect in taking us north to gain more sea room. We were being pushed slowly towards the rocky reef-fringed shore and there was precisely nothing that I could do about it. As we slowly edged in closer to the shore, I began to search desperately for some sandy beach that fronted a small village, where we could hope for some help to bring *Hermes* in.

We began to make preparations for an emergency beaching. All the fenders were brought out from the stern locker ready to lash around the bows and the keel. But the more I looked for a suitable beach, the more worried I became. Rocks, the odd patch of shingle—nowhere along the whole coast was there a safe sandy beach. As a last resort, when we were a few hundred yards off a shingle beach, I decided to drop anchor. With luck it would hold us until the storm and seas had abated. At least it would slow us down as we approached the shore.

Two hundred yards from the shore, I yelled to Dave to let the anchor go. It plummeted downwards to a depth of over 200 feet. Slowly we were washed in towards the breakers pounding onto the hard stony beach. Then it caught. It slackened again. It caught once more and *Hermes* swung her bows into the seas. We were less than 100 yards from the shore.

Our troubles were not yet over. I awoke in the early hours of the morning to the sound of surf smashing on rocks. At first I thought it could be a bad dream, but when I raised my head a few inches, I looked out into the darkness astern and saw jagged rocks of coral facing upwards through the swirling seas. 'Haul in the anchor while I start the motor,' I yelled to Dave who was keeping an anchor watch. We plugged into the steep-running swirl out into deeper water. 'Right, drop anchor,' I yelled, taking the motor out of gear so that *Hermes* would drift into the shore. The reef came closer and still we did not stop. 'Is the anchor holding?' I called to Dave.

'It's not down.'

'For fuck's sake why not?'

'Because I didn't fucking well hear you.'

I slammed the outboard into gear to run back out to sea. Fifty yards from the coral *Hermes* suddenly came to a jarring halt. 'Have we hit something?' I called anxiously to Dave.

'No. I dropped the anchor back nearer the shore.'

'For Christ's sake open your ears,' I screamed. 'Now pull that bloody anchor in and don't throw it over until you have repeated my orders.'

A mumbled reply from the fore deck. The manoeuvre was repeated, this time successfully, and *Hermes* rode to the anchor fifty yards farther seaward. At first light I looked out again. All was well and the storm had abated.

The continued strain and tension, with the perpetual storms and reef-strewn waters, were beginning to take their toll. Off watch, at night, I found I could hardly sleep. I would toss and turn until eventually, through complete fatigue, I would fall into a spasmodic sleep, only to be awoken by some bad dream or nightmare—of *Hermes* being dragged onto some sharp coral reef; or a storm suddenly developing, fierce winds tearing at *Hermes'* sails and capsizing her, casting us into the shark-infested waters.

Inevitably Dave found himself on the receiving end of my outbursts. A few days later we used the last of the light land breezes to take us out into the Sumba Strait and across to the island of Flores. Our provisions and fresh water were again running desperately short, and I noticed on the chart a small village called Reo situated in a bay of the same name, fifty miles eastwards along the north coast of Flores. As we approached the bay, late that night, a strong southerly wind began to blow down from the mountains. We reduced sail and I beat *Hermes* in through a steep choppy sea. Two hours later and five miles from Reo river, it was time to change watch; I handed over to Dave, while I went below the canopy to try and get some sleep. At six the following morning, when I was due to come back on watch, I looked out towards the land. It was only a shadowy outline against the rising sun. We were now over ten miles from the bay.

By failing to sail as efficiently as possible, Dave had allowed the boat to drift farther to seawards with the strong headwinds. I was cold, wet and tired and for the first time in ten months I let fly, only to regret it a few minutes later. He had done his best; he just lacked experience, or so I kept reminding myself over the next four hours, as I beat *Hermes* back into Reo Bay and towards the mouth of the river.

We sailed up the muddy waters of the river, through the mixture of mango swamps and palm trees, towards the village. Four dug-out canoes, with two or three children in each, came in swiftly from the bay and joined us. They were the friendliest and most cheerful children I had ever met. They paddled alongside, laughing and shouting and peering curiously into *Hermes*. We arrived to find over 100 villagers gathered around the banks to see us come in. When I stepped ashore with papers and passports, I was immediately greeted in perfect English by the local school-teacher, Hendrikus Nala, who took me along to the local police post. The formalities were quickly dealt with and we set off in search of provisions.

Hendrikus took us to a Chinese friend of his called Go Tjung Hoa, or Tjungy. Before we knew what was happening, we were invited into his

The after deck, crossing the Timor Sea;
life-raft emergency rations in bag, and emergency water going green with mould

Flying fish on board—crossing the Timor Sea

At Darwin pier

Two Australian aborigines: on the left the old man is smoking a pipe made from a crab's claw; the right-hand man has a patch of skin grafted onto his chest

home, a large wooden bungalow, and seated at a table that was groaning under a huge spread of various fish and vegetables. Before the hospitality got out of hand, I decided to ask about the fuel which we so desperately needed. He quoted 100 rupees a litre. As soon as he saw my face he lowered the price to seventy-five rupees, which was more reasonable. With that out of the way, we got down to the serious business of eating.

A German mission post, set half a mile within the jungle, was the only brick building within Reo. We spent the night at the mission, having left *Hermes* moored alongside the muddy river bank. In the early hours I was awoken by a small boy who said that there had been heavy rains up in the hills and that the river was in full flood. I slipped on a shirt and sarong, hardly relishing the thought of the half-mile walk back through the jungle in pitch blackness. Until now I had only heard the jungle at night from the safety of *Hermes*. Now it completely enveloped me, unnervingly close. But after about fifty yards I began to feel strangely relaxed. I was completely cut off from the tensions and stresses of our western so-called civilisation, and yet I felt at home. When we reached *Hermes*, we found that she was in no danger. I laid out a few more mooring warps, in case the river should rise any farther, before returning to the mission.

What was intended as an afternoon stop extended to a number of days, while the hospitality we received became almost an embarrassment. We ate in Tjungy's house and ate well—massive spreads of meats, rice, vegetables, fish and fruit. According to Hendrikus, Tjungy was the wealthiest Chinese merchant in Reo. His house was at the far end of the muddy main street, and constructed of old wooden planks and corrugated iron sheeting. It served both as his home and as his store. He also owned a small farm ten miles along the coast, where he had 1000 coconut palms for the production of copra. He drove us out there one day in his Jeep, all around the northwestern corner of Flores. He was a rare character, wealthy yet generous to a fault. When we paid him roughly £10 for fuel, he insisted on giving us about £15 worth of sarongs.

Within a few days I found that I was beginning to slip into the idyllic way of life—easy-going and unashamedly, luxuriously simple—but Dave had other ideas. He wanted to get going, to reach Australia as fast as possible. Whilst we were in Reo his whole temperament seemed to change. We were always followed, for example, by a group of children; they meant no harm and I could understand their curiosity. They had never met a white man before. One day while we were both on board *Hermes*, they came down and sat on her gunwales. 'Why don't the little perishers leave us alone?' Dave began to growl.

'They're all right,' I said, 'they're only curious.' I started chatting to them and soon discovered that with one exception they were all Christians. So I pulled out the ship's Bible, which was illustrated with a number of coloured photographs of various holy places through the Middle East. The children were enthralled and chatted excitedly. They had heard of all the names, but they had never seen photographs before. It was getting late in the afternoon and the dark rain clouds appeared on cue, to give us the regular afternoon downpour. The children all clambered on board to shelter underneath the canopy.

'Watch where you're putting your feet,' Dave shouted.

'Easy on, Dave, they're doing no harm,' I said.

Hendrikus, our school-teacher friend who was always with us, took me to one side later and asked what was wrong. The Indonesian people love their children, and he could not understand Dave's attitude. I told him that it was probably the heat.

Unfortunately the time came when we had to leave, since the southeast monsoon was already threatening.

Before we left, Tjungy also helped us out with another problem that was beginning to worry us. If we took Nell to Australia, there was a chance that she would run into trouble with the health officials. She had become part of the crew and part of us—the last thing in our minds was to see her hurt and never, if we could possibly help it, destroyed. Tjungy, like most Chinese, was very fond of cats. His own cat had the run of the house; whereas the dog was a mangy beast, scrawny and covered in scars, the cat was fat and healthy. We decided that here was the best home we could ever expect to find for Nell; with considerable sadness I handed her over. She was tired of voyaging. When we were close to land, she would look longingly at the shore, and often break into a pitiful wail. It was, we were

sure, the best thing for her, and she seemed very happy with the arrange-
ment—Tjungy's cat was a tom!

A large number of the villagers came down to see us off. Many of them
had become friends, and I felt sad at having to say goodbye so soon. As
we prepared for a 400-mile voyage to Dili, in Portuguese Timor, I promised Hendrikus and Tjungy that I would definitely return one day, another
promise that I have every intention of keeping.

For six days there wasn't a hint of steady measurable wind, either from
the north-west or south-east. At night we hugged the shore as close as we
dared, to gain what land breeze there might be. In the mornings we lay
becalmed in an oily smooth sea, waiting for a light breeze in the afternoon
to waft us slowly eastwards. The days were hot and muggy, and when
off watch we would sit on the fore-deck dousing ourselves with buckets
of cool sea water. Any thoughts of diving in over the side were soon dis-
pelled. At regular intervals every day we could sight a menacing triangular
fin carving through the deep blue waters.

We made a point of washing as much of our clothing as possible during
this period, since much of it was green with mould after months of being
stored in the forward locker. We looked a strange sight with shirts, sweaters, underpants and shorts hanging in the rigging. To try and counteract
the boredom and frustration of this leg to Dili, I tried every possible sail
combination, to obtain just a fraction of a knot more in speed. We rigged
up a form of spinnaker, made from six panels of a bright yellow parachute,
as a leg-of-mutton trysail between the mizzen and main, and the forward
gap was filled in with the mosquito net. Sporting this strange rig, we would
often be visited by native fishing craft, whose crews would peer with undy-
ing curiosity at such a peculiar craft from a far-away land.

After rounding the eastern end of Alor island, I set a southeasterly
course through the Ombat Strait to Dili, Portuguese Timor, which we
sighted at sunrise on 21 March. At first sight the harbour seemed to be
completely open with little or no protection from the north-west monsoon, but as we sailed through the narrow entrance I realised that this was
a natural harbour, fringed by a coral reef submerged at high water.

Lying close in to the beach to port, I noticed a large black ketch, obviously well travelled, with a self-steering vane swinging loosely to the light northerly wind. 'Looks like another world voyager,' said Dave, who then dived into the starboard locker and brought out the binoculars. '*Sea Wanderer*.'

'That's Eddie Alcard's boat!' I exclaimed. 'I never expected to meet up with him. Small world.'

I sailed up alongside a concrete wharf. After we had obtained our medical and customs clearance, I noticed a familiar bearded figure, pushing an unfamiliar pram. I shouted a greeting and Eddie came over.

He looked down at us hard. Eddie's boat was thirty times the displacement of *Hermes*. When I told him that we would be crossing the Timor Sea to Australia in a few days, he slowly shook his head. 'Rather you than me. But come over if you are free this evening. We'd be glad to take you out for a meal.'

'We?' I said, looking at the pram.

'Yes,' he laughed. 'My wife and I were married in New Zealand just over a year ago. She flies out with our baby daughter and meets me wherever I happen to stop for any length of time.'

'Good idea!' murmured Dave.

The town of Dili was typically Portuguese, in architecture and cleanliness; but the inhabitants were far removed from the Malay type of Indonesians. Their complexion was darker, almost negroid; with their lack of oriental charm, they seemed nearer to the Australian Abos. They were desperately poor, and not very cheerful about it. Dave and I found a shaded cafe. 'Whatever happens,' I said, 'we must cross the Timor Sea as fast as possible.'

The south-east monsoon was almost upon us and the majority of winds would be from that direction. What's more the cyclone season had arrived; according to the pilot guide, the cyclones were pretty frequent. The outboard still seemed to be working well; obviously we were going to have to rely heavily on this during the next week or ten days. We also reviewed the cash situation. 'We've about £20 sterling left between us. £10 will buy us 50 gallons of fuel and oil, £5 for provisions and the other £5 for when we arrive in Australia. O.K.?' 'O.K. Let's go.'

We spent the following two hours moving from one garage to the next, trying to find extra containers for the massive amount of fuel we had to buy. We staggered back to *Hermes* under a pile of five-litre paraffin cans, two-, five- and 10-litre bottles and a few burnt-out paint tins.

By a happy coincidence, it was my birthday. It was a kind thought on Eddie's part to have us over for a meal, and we spent a most enjoyable time talking boats, discussing the problems we might meet across the Timor Sea. 'You'll meet a mass of electric storms,' he warned. 'More severe than any you may have encountered through the Indonesian islands. I was caught on the hop once and it laid me flat. So keep a good look out and be ready for when they hit!' I tried to look unconcerned. We had 500 miles to go before Darwin, anything upwards of a week away. Australia seemed so near, yet so far.

The following day, after a thorough check of the outboard and transmitter, we paid our final respects to the crew of *Sea Wanderer*, and left Dili, sailing before a light north-westerly. By the next afternoon we were sheltering under a headland from a strong easterly. I listened to the radio for a weather report from Darwin, and the announcer confirmed my suspicions, namely that a cyclone was travelling through northern Australia. I tried contacting Darwin, which was 400 miles away as the crow flies, but no one answered. The wind continued to blow and to break the frustration of waiting we stripped off for a swim. Just as we were about to leap over the side, I noticed, ten yards off, a school of bonito leaping out of the water. Then four triangular fins broke surface and began to dart amongst them. Without a word we both sat down again in the cockpit. I reached back for a ten-litre bottle of cheap Portuguese red wine, as the sharks went into the attack.

When we were ten miles south of the island of Leti I tried radioing Darwin once more, but no one replied. Just as I was about to give up, the receiver crackled into life.

'Hullo, *Hermes* calling Australia, this is the tug *John Ingam* bound for Singapore. Can we help you ? Over.'

I leaped for the handset. 'Hullo, *John Ingam*, this is British yacht *Hermes*, I am trying to get a weather report for crossing the Timor Sea.

Over.' The tug passed on their last report, for pretty good weather, light south-easterlies, no storm warnings, for which I thanked them. Then they asked me for our position, which I gave them. There was a pause for half a minute, before the tug came through again.

'Hullo, *Hermes*, would you like to meet up with us? We are ninety miles east-south-east of you, at a position twenty miles south of Sermata island approximately. Over.'

'Romeo, *John Ingam*, we'd love to meet up, what's your course and speed please? Over.'

Again there was a short pause, then, 'Our course is 284 true, and speed 4½ knots. Over.'

'Romeo, *John Ingam*, standby please, I'll be back to you soon.' I pulled out the chart and plotted their position relative to ours and drew on it a converging course. If we motored we could maintain a speed of 4 knots also. I picked up the handset and told them what course we would be steering and that we should meet up around 2300 hours. We agreed to keep a regular hourly schedule.

The wind was blowing light from the south-east so we hauled down the sails and started the outboard, and I brought *Hermes* round on her new course. Every hour we established contact with the tug and reported our relative positions, course and speed. The *John Ingam* was towing a 15,000-ton oil rig and had been on the move from the Bass Straits for over six weeks. They were only too pleased to have something to break the monotony; we, too, were feeling a bit lonesome. 'Never know. They might even offer us a meal,' I said.

At the 2130 hours radio schedule we had not sighted the tug and I was beginning to wonder if my navigation was at fault. 'We'll turn on our searchlights and flash them up to the clouds,' the tug's radio operator suggested. Dave and I peered into the darkness. Suddenly the sky was lit up with powerful beams of light arcing across the skies. 'We see you, *John Ingam*,' I said excitedly, 'dead on course.' Our actual meeting time was 2250 hours, only ten minutes out from my ETA. A smaller tug was detached from the massive oil rig and came across. I brought *Hermes* alongside and we laid her astern.

Within minutes Dave and I were tucking into a huge meal of steak and eggs in the tug's galley. As we were sitting there, with the yolks of the eggs dripping from our chins, the tug's crew, consisting mainly of British chaps and a few Australians, began to pack a mass of provisions into a sack and two cardboard boxes. 'There yer ar', cock, yer can stuff yerselves stupid on that lot,' said one of the crew with a strong cockney accent. 'Well, I'll hand it to yer, it's only the fucking British that could be so bloody mad as to do what yer doin'.'

The total was enough for two month's supplies, with cooked hams, smoked sausage, tins of fresh milk, bread, butter, tinned meats, chickens, and goodness knows what else. After we had been on board for an hour the main convoy was given miles to the east and the tug skipper was becoming a little concerned; Dave and I staggered off with the mass of provisions, which filled *Hermes*' cockpit to overflowing. The crew released our tow line, and we slowly slipped astern.

As we watched her disappear into the darkness, we both sensed a feeling of utter loneliness, of how small we were on a sea frequented only by liners and large ocean tugs. But at least we would be well fed in our isolation, thanks to the skipper and crew of the *John Ingam*.

For the next four days we motored steadily southwards. To my great relief the wind was virtually non-existent; at night, fierce electric storms would flicker and flash all around, the dull roar of thunder rumbling across the sea, but none of them came close enough to cause us any alarm. All the same, navigating was a major cause for worry. My sextant had packed up two months before, due to water getting behind the mirrors. We were sailing towards almost uncharted waters, and with only a dead reckoning position to go on. Darwin had a radio beacon and I took a continuous DF bearing on this, but it was the only station and the best I could do was to take a series of running fixes. The speed of the current through the Arafura and Timor Seas is very erratic at this time of the year, and I had to guess the surface current's speed from wind observation.

On 29March the log read: 'ESTABLISHED CONTACT WITH DARWIN RADIO AT 1330 HOURS LOCAL TIME. RECEIVED WEATHER REPORT — LIGHT S.E. WINDS ISOLATED THUNDER STORMS. FUEL RAN OUT AT 1330 HOURS. DEAD RECKONING

POSITION 40 MILES NORTH OF BATHURST ISLAND, WIND CALM.' For the rest of that afternoon we rolled in a long glassy swell; the sails hung limp, the sun beat down from a clear sky and we sat sweltering under the sun awning, waiting for wind. Early evening brought a breeze from the west, the sails filled and we gathered speed. Just before sunset I climbed the mainmast and searched the southern horizon for land, but saw nothing.

With darkness the wind freshened, veering slightly to the northwest. I was sure land wasn't far off; Bathurst Island is a low-lying bed of mangrove swamps, and there was little chance of sighting it from more than fifteen miles off. I altered course slightly to the southwest and began to work furiously on a mass of figures to estimate where we were and when we should be close to land. Our speed was five knots, and I estimated that if we sailed on this course for six hours it would put us approximately five miles off the northwestern tip of Bathurst Island. We could then alter course due eastwards, under reduced sail, and slowly close in slightly northwards of the island. Mermaid shoal extended ten miles northwards of the island, which, although marked as insufficiently charted, did have one or two soundings of $1\frac{1}{2}$ fathoms. We could soon tell if we were going over the shoal by the state of the sea. We could drop anchor and await daybreak to find our position.

Throughout my watch I sailed a course slightly west of south and handed over to Dave giving him instructions to wake me after the first two hours. When the time came we hove to and looked towards the southeast, peering into the pitch blackness of the night, hoping to see land with the help of the flashes of lightning from a near-by storm. Nothing. I went forward and lowered the mainsail, and gave Dave a due easterly course to steer, warning him that we must be close and to keep a good lookout.

An hour and a half later he woke me to say that he thought he could see a dark line to southward. I came out from under the canopy and immediately smelled land. The wind had backed to the south-west and was blowing quite fresh. I untied the sea anchor on the after deck and added six fathoms of chain and 200 feet of nylon warp, and took it up to the fore deck. I heaved it overboard and waited for *Hermes* to take up the strain but the warp just lay on the surface. I hauled it in and found that it was on the bottom. 'It's shallow here,' I shouted, pulling in the sea anchor. I unshackled it and attached the warp and chain to the ground anchor on the fore deck and threw that overboard. It hit bottom in only six feet of water.

By the time the sails were furled and all was shipshape once more on board, dawn began to break. There was no mistaking it, land was five miles to southward. A low line of mangrove trees, a desolate, deserted, uninhabited shoreline. 'Well, there's Australia,' I said, 'but where in Australia, God knows. It's either Bathurst or Melville Island, but I'll be damned if I know which.' For half an hour I studied the chart and the shoreline, trying to find some identifiable point to fix our position. I guessed that we were to the north of Cape Van Diemen, the north-western part of Melville Island. 'If we sail around that cape we should end up in the straits between Melville and Bathurst Islands.'

As we rounded the cape, I realised that my estimate had been right. The wide open stretch of water called Apsley Strait showed up, dividing the land in two. We sailed towards it, beating hard into a strong south-westerly, hoping that this uncharted shoal that we were sailing over had no uncharted rocks. The wind died on us as we entered the sheltered waters of the strait, and we dropped anchor for the night.

Early in the morning of 2 April 1970 we sighted Darwin. I transmitted a short telegram to be sent on to my father, 'ARRIVED OFF DARWIN 0100 HOURS GMT, ALL WELL.' For the first time ever an open boat had sailed from England to Australia. After a year of both joy and suffering, in excess of anything we had experienced ever before in our lives, we had made it.

*   *   *   *   *

Half an hour after clearing customs Dave and I were busy tidying the boat when we heard an unmistakable twang from the jetty above us. Looking up, we saw a middle-aged blonde with her two scruffy kids.

'England—Australia,' one of the boys piped up, reading the legend off the side of *Hermes*.

'England's a long way, innit, Ma?' the other squeaked.

'Gam, the two of you,' the lady replied. 'England—Australia, my foot;

bet they bloody shipped that little boat out on a liner, and got themselves dropped off outside the harbour.'

For a fleeting second, I was tempted to fire a broadside back at the dear lady. I looked at Dave, who was grinning like a Cheshire cat. 'Would have been easier, though, wouldn't it?' he said quietly.